Declutter Workbook Step by Step

How to organize your Life and Home with a Practical Decluttering Guide and Simple Cleaning Exercises to Grow Daily Stress-Free Mind Habits to Get Rid of Anxiety

by Rebecca Larsson

TABLE OF CONTENTS

Introduction

Today we live in a world of abundance. Income levels are up, unemployment is down, education is up. Never before has there been an amount of opportunities for the average person to live a comfortable lifestyle. The commercialization of popular goods means that the market is flooded with different products that consumers can spend their hard earned cash on. We go to work, come home and spend, spend, spend when the direct deposit hits our bank account. There was a time when somebody's status was equated with the amount of stuff they could buy and fit into their homes. But our homes have now become overcrowded with so many things that we forget they are even there.

A messy home sounds harmless at first glance, but it can be a serious problem. Even when the state of the house is manageable there are some points that should be considered. Is your work area or desk kept clean? Does every object in your home have its own place? What about the kitchen and living areas? Is there enough room to feel at ease with yourself and your surroundings?

Your answers to these questions will vary across different personality types and lifestyles. There are those who are highly organized, and then there are those who just let things lay where they may. Sometimes a messy home can really start to bother someone and turn into a problem. Others won't seem to care. Maybe someone is too busy because of work and other commitments that they can't be as organized. But chances are since you picked up this book, you know that there is a problem in your organizational skills and that you want to remove the clutter.

The accumulation of things in the home can have a real impact on your mental well-being. The overabundance of things you can see but that you don't actually use may cause you to feel overwhelmed, anxious, and trapped inside your home. As humans, we have a tendency to find uses for things, whether in the future or in the immediate moment. The things that are collected throughout the home are like tiny little promises you have made to yourself.

For example, if you collect different mugs, you may feel like you have to use them at some point. And if you don't, dust begins to accumulate on the neglected merchandise. Every time you look at those mugs you feel a sense of betrayal to yourself, but also a sense that you have left things unfinished. Nobody likes this feeling. It's as if you have backlogged yourself with a set of tasks that you don't have them for. So what can we do? We substitute pushing things away for cleaning. We hide the mugs in the cupboards, behind the shelves and wherever else we can stuff them.

Instead of dealing with the problem we like to put it off for as long as possible. And over time what started as a few innocent decisions later results in drastic changes to the house. Those changes in turn can affect your mood. The house becomes full of useless trinkets that you no longer know what to do with. Even when you try to tidy things up you realize that there isn't enough space in your home to put things away. You just end up moving things around into garages, attics, storage units, and backyard sheds.

These are all temporary problems to a chronic condition, one that needs to be nipped in the bud for good. If you suffer from this problem and it is not corrected, you run the risk of losing the house to refuse. Well, not really. Most clutter is just clutter. You clean it up and it's gone. But there are certain bad habits that tend to make the problem worse. When those habits aren't fixed the clutter will always return like a pesky uninvited guest. And nobody wants that. A home should remain manageable and clutter-free year round.

In Japan there is a phenomenon called the trash house where a house can become so unkempt that trash bags literally pile up to the walls. These are households where the owners have either let themselves go or who are too elderly to take care of themselves. They can also be abandoned places where people have decided to dump their trash illegally. Houses were not meant to be filled up to the brim. At that point they become unlivable. The purpose of the house is defeated. Strangely enough some people live in these conditions, and not just in Japan. The phenomena are observable all around the world.

The vast majority of people who deal with clutter are not destined to live in trash houses. They are ordinary people who simply have too much stuff and don't know what to do with it. People who, feel dissatisfied after cleaning their homes because there may still be a mess of things leftover. No matter how much they scrub, broom or reorganize the home it still becomes self-evident that they simply have too much stuff.

These sorts of situations arise when there isn't enough help around the house or when people are caught up at work with little free time. They also arise when people have some mechanism for acquiring things in the first place, which will be talked about in later chapters. These mechanisms are bad habits that lead to the pursuit of collecting objects. They could be clothes, kitchenware, electronics, toys, nick knacks, and things of that nature.

In a way the act of collecting things is an outdated habit. We live in a world of abundance. If something is lost or stolen you can easily replace them. If something is needed around the house you can visit the nearest department store. Putting things inside the house is easy. Taking them out is more complicated Objects create a burden once inside the home. They hold a strange gravity to them.

They are difficult to get rid of and drive people crazy. Your relationships may suffer, and you may start to develop mental health issues like anxiety and depression. In contrast, a clean home that is orderly and has a nice balance of space, utility and beauty will fire up your creative circuits and give you energy. Not only will you feel at home, but you will also feel free to express yourself and to be productive.

Everyone knows the saying that "your body is your temple", but few pay heed to how important your physical home, your actual temple, can be. The home is where the heart is. It is where we spend the majority of our time outside of work or school. The home is a reflection of our social and personal lives. They are also where our families and significant others spent most of their time. In those cases, the home isn't just about you, but about a collective group of individuals all living under the same roof. And when clutter starts to pile up, everyone is affected. It's not just you who feels anxious, but the entire household.

The home is sacred, but we are sometimes too busy to pay attention to it. We occupy time and space but we spend most of our time somewhere else, living inside of our heads. After five o' clock we might be in the house, or on our way to work. In the early morning most of us are just stirring out of bed.

During all of these situations we are also inside of our heads—that is, in our own consciousness. And while we can have a time and place to match our locality, the fact that we think to ourselves means that we are always inside our personal bubble.

If the home can become cluttered so too can the mind. There is a connection between the organization of our mind and the organization of the home. Objects reflect into our thoughts by creating a sense of urgency. Like if something is always left undone.

One of the easiest ways to dump this cognitive load is to lessen the clutter inside the home. Your mind becomes decoupled from the spurious objects that surround you at all times and you can breathe again. Your mind can focus on other things, and be left alone to wander. Being mindful of your actions goes a long way towards decluttering your mind, and mindfulness is difficult to achieve when your senses are assaulted on all fronts by the clutter inside the home.

This book offers a step by step program to begin reversing the bad habits that have plagued you and your home with clutter. It doesn't matter where these habits came from, or for how long they have been affecting you. In time you can work wonders to combat them. All that you need is a little forward motion to get changes done and the correct formula for making these changes stick for the long term.

Chapter One will introduce what this formula for success is and what it looks like in your daily life. Note that change doesn't happen overnight, or that you can make changes on a whim. Change starts by moving small things, making small decisions and being mindful. Over time these small things turn into results.

Then in Chapter Two you will explore the different ways that the formula can be broken down into maintainable parts. Creating a step by step process makes it easier to commit over a long term. At the end of the tunnel you will be rewarded with a cleaner, more harmonious house and an unburdened mind.

The topic of mindfulness and awareness of the self is covered in Chapter Three. Often times we make decisions about the home without being fully aware that we are doing them. We introduce new objects into the house, thinking that there will be a place for them. Not because you made the proper record keeping to make sure that this object belongs, but because you simply thought the object was needed. Being mindful of needs will prevent extra objects from entering the home.

Chapter Four explains how to get a hold of your organizational deficit and turn it on its head. This deficit is made up of the decisions that you make (whether consciously or not) to populate your home with things. Some of us are natural born organizers, most of us are not. Since you are reading this book, you probably fall under the latter. But that can easily be fixed.

Chapter Five is all about indecisiveness, and the inability to make decisions on the spot. Sometimes we don't know what to do with objects. We want to hold on to them, even though we know we need to make space in the house. We become indecisive, and are unable to say yes or no to the simplest questions. The result? Nothing gets tossed. Nothing gets organized.

Cleaning the house—and keeping it that way—is made up of a system. Thinking in terms of systems and systemic ways of keeping things in order is talked about in Chapter Six. Then in Chapter Seven you will be introduced to different mental models that will help you think critically about the cleaning process.

Chapter Eight offers some specifics about keeping the house spotless and how to actually clean. For example, every room requires its own set of cleaning techniques and organizational requirements. No two rooms are created equal in this sense. Finally chapter Nine will condense the contents of this book into a cohesive package and program that you can follow. This is all about going from disharmony to harmonious living and staying that way.

Chapter 1: The Formula

"Mens sana in corpore sano" - Latin phrase

In mathematics certain problems are solvable by following a formula to derive the answer. Formulas are battle-tested, methodically sound steps towards a logical conclusion. The problem facing you is a disorganized home that doesn't radiate harmony. What we mean by this is that the home becomes a source of stress rather than strength. Note also that the problem doesn't have to be in the scope of a complete dumpster fire. Your problem can be a slight disharmony in the available space you have. It could also be a phobia of throwing things away, or a tendency to collect useless items that provide no use. Whatever the case, rest assured that there is a formula for arriving at the solution for any of these issues.

The above Latin phrase "Mens sana in corpore sano" is translated to mean "A healthy mind inside a healthy body". It's an old proverb, historically used to celebrate the power of exercise in conjunction with the power of the brain. As we all know, the Romans where big fans of sport. To them it wasn't enough to have a healthy mind. One also needed to have a healthy body. This can further be traced to the Greeks when Aristotle said that physical strength and wellness was a type of virtue, just like being a kind and honorable person was also a virtue.

The Greeks and Romans believed that a person was not whole unless both the mind and the body were regularly exercised. In other words, both aspects of the human condition were seen as vitally important to society. Though this book argues that they also missed a third factor that is just as important, and that is having an orderly environment. One then can extend this quote to say "A healthy mind inside a healthy body inside an orderly home". It sounds a bit contrived, but if the body influences the mind and if the mind influences the body, there is an argument to be said that the home also affects these things. After all, the body is found somewhere within time and space. Everything affects everything else. And since we spend a large portion of our time within the home, it makes sense that the state of the home can have a profound effect on our mind.

When there is a disconnect between the three you begin to sense a problem: a messy home influences behavior, which influences mental state. When the house is a mess the law of inertia tends to gain control. The messier it is, the less likely you are to start cleaning. One messy habit begets another. You begin to eat on the couch, and instead of taking your plate to the sink you leave it lying around. You don't want to cook anything so you order out. More bags, plastic containers and utensils, more trash, and more things that you don't want to pick up.

As a consequence you no longer sit up straight. You begin to slouch. Instead of reaching for the napkins you smear the Cheeto dust on your pants. Instead of trying to learn new things or try new experiences you rather stay home. You aren't interested in starting projects after work, or pursuing your hobbies. You would rather sit in the muck of your living room and go on your phone. Or at least, that's how the logic goes. A breakdown in one area causes a chain reaction. A messy home becomes a messy body, which becomes a messy mind.

This isn't a pretty picture by any means. And yet during certain times in our lives we feel that we are going down that route. Most of us are able to bounce back. Even if we do bounce back, some of the bad habits remain and we are constantly at odds with them.

The potential chain reaction that stems from a disorganized home is the problem that we are trying to fix. Because if you stop the problem at the root, you have a good chance of avoiding the chain reaction that follows. To fight this problem we need to first understand how it is created, thereby creating a formula to reserve it.

The Four Truths of Decluttering

So what exactly is behind the chain reaction? There is a little something called human nature and the set of behaviors that go with it. Not only that, but there is a scenario called modern life. When you put both human nature and modern life together you get a recipe for disaster that is in many ways difficult to address. We are only partially to blame for the house getting disorderly.

1. Disorganized People Are Messy

Let's face it. Someone who isn't actively involved in the organization of their home is going to run into problems. But it also doesn't mean they should give up and that their house is doomed. They will simply struggle a little bit more to keep their houses clean in comparison to someone who takes organization seriously. The good news is that organizational skills can be learned at no great personal cost. The only thing it takes is a little bit of courage to unlearn old habits and to be mindful in everything that you do.

Disorganization can be a symptom of a bigger problem. Laziness can sometimes be confused for disorganization, for example and vice versa. If somebody doesn't have the time to slow down and be a little organized they might even be suffering from some addiction or preoccupation that prevents them from taking the time to organize.

Know that there is a cost to just about anything you do. When buying new things there is a cost in terms of space and energy associated with the purchase. Not just the money in wages that they cost you, but now the psychological burden of having them in your home. Likewise there is a cost associated with your actions. Failure to wash the dishes on one day means you will have double the work on the next.

2. Mess Is a Result of Disorganization

Another word for disorganization here is carelessness. If somebody doesn't care they are not going to put things away where they belong (or even designate areas for certain things). A house doesn't become a dumpster by itself. It is the result of careless actions taken by the people who live inside it. Dirty floors and soiled walls don't occur spontaneously. Over time there may be a built up of dust and other debris as time tends to make these things happen. But that is the natural course of occupying any space. It is up to the occupants of that space to clean up and maintain the household when chaos occurs.

Because disorganization is also a habit, it pays to pay attention to what you are doing. It is far too easy today to leave things for later and then completely forget about them. Practicing mindfulness and being aware of how objects fit within your home is key. Otherwise things will get messy and they will stay that away unless something is done.

There is also a selection problem at work. A person can be disorganized on the surface, but say that they are the most organized person you have met. They may point at a bag and say "that one has a bunch of toys" and "that one over there is full of swimming shorts. I might need those one day". Where you see a mess they see complete order.

This is essentially a problem of selection, meaning that the focus is on the smaller details. The disorganized person might feel like they are control because each object has a perceived utility to them. They chose to ignore everything else.

This is either wishful thinking or self delusion. Nobody needs to keep all the things that they think they need. Those future scenarios where objects "might" be needed are unlikely to happen in reality. And if those scenarios do occur, the economy we live in is usually liquid enough that we can simply go out and buy what is needed, rather than saving it indefinitely.

The selection problem is a failure to make prudent decisions about what should be kept and what should be discarded. Better yet, it is a problem of gauging the things someone needs. Knowing what your needs are and how those needs change can help avoid the problem.

3. Humans Have Infinite Wants But Limited Space

The economy is booming. Social mobility is at an all time high. If someone wants a better job all they have to do is apply themselves, get new skills and advance up the social ladder. Acquiring new skills has never been easier since the Internet came online. More and more consumer products are hitting the market at breakneck speeds. The rise of fast fashion retailers has also drastically reduced the price of designer clothes. Some of these clothes are so low quality that they need to be replaced after a few uses.

Unfortunately, humans are needy. Most of us like shiny things, and buying new products at the mall is a big form of stress relief. Retail therapy as it has been called, causes an influx of new items entering your home. Since we shop to feel good, many of these products are not useful the way other products are. We buy, buy, buy without being aware of what we already have, what we need, and especially where we are going to put everything.

There is a saying that the bigger the house, the more junk that fits inside it. If you feel overwhelmed about the available space in your home, buying a bigger home would probably not solve the problem. In time that house would also become crowded. Why? Because you aren't targeting the root cause. The sooner you understand that space is always limited compared to our infinite desires then the quicker you will be able to live in harmony with having fewer things. If anything, buying a smaller house would more likely fix the issue because then you are forced to throw things out.

4. Everyone Is Different

No two snowflakes are exactly alike. And people are infinitely more complex than snowflakes. Some of us like to collect things, others are fine owning only a few possessions. Some would balk at the idea of owning only five changes of clothes, and yet some are perfectly happy wearing the same thing their entire lives.

That everybody is different, with slightly different needs, requires that we have more than one formula. The formula needs to be tweaked according to the person. Some people are rich in money, others rich in time. Some in both, some in neither. If the end goal is to live a harmonious life within the home, changes need to be done based on the unique circumstances the individual finds themselves in.

And if you thought people being different was bad, the issue gets further complicated if you consider how households are different. Some people live alone, others have small families. Or they have big families. Some people who live alone receive assistance from family members. Others do not. Some live with adults, others with small children who cannot take care of their selves.

Maintaining a clean house doesn't have to be a lone enterprise. If you have a spouse you should split up chores evenly. Older and young children alike can also do chores around the house. At the bare minimum, they should be responsible for cleaning their own room and looking after any pets.

No Problem Too Big

We are the sum of our habits. Both the good and the bad. Habits are given such great consideration throughout this book because they have the ability to change lives. For better, or for worse. Bad habits will be given special focus because they are the harbingers of all disorder in the home. For every good habit that you have the bad one will stand out more. We remember negative experiences more than positive ones.

The bigger the problem, the more effort it took to grow that big. People have little screw-ups throughout their lives and come out just fine. But when those screw-ups happen all the time and

nothing is done to address them, people can really destroy their lives. The same thing goes for home. A steady trickle of bad habits will create a deeper problem.

Peace is never made overnight. There are no easy "hacks" to get your house in order in a short amount of time. So if you are planning a big dinner at your house and expect shortcuts, then forget it. Take a moment to visualize what the problem is. How did you get here? And where do you think you are going from this point? You can either move forward or go backwards. You can regress or you can triumph. Big problems are made out of tiny ones. If you can identify and reverse those small impurities then you can overcome any problem. No problem is too big.

A mountain can be moved by clearing a stone everyday. Little by little the stones accumulate, and the mountain is eventually gone. The most important part of the formula then, is to break things down into manageable chunks. The idea is not to clean your house in one go, but to foster a healthy way of living that keeps the house clean throughout the year.

Once you understand the four truths you can begin formulating your attack plan. First up are your organization skills. If they need some work then that is where you will start. Objects inside your house should belong with other like objects, and so on. Your desk should not be a bunch of papers strewn all over. You should be able to put things away after using them—as well as everyone else in your home.

Second is the mess that results from disorganization. A messy house tends to stay messy and a clean house tends to stay clean. Understand that by lifting the first stone towards moving the mountain you will build the necessary momentum to keep going.

Third is the space situation. Here you will have to make the important decisions over what stays and what goes. The result will vary on what available space you have and how much you value that space. While it is possible to cover every inch of your house with stuff and still do it in a neat fashion, most people are better off getting rid of extra and unused things. For the sanity of your mind space is always king.

Finally, you will have to address these things under the confines of your unique situation. This is the hardest part, as it incorporates everything else. There is also no set path that will guarantee success for any one person. You will have to figure this out through trial and error.

But don't worry. You don't have to have answers to these things just yet. The rest of the chapters in this book will help you decide what space means to you, what objects really matter, and how to put it together for your benefit. Along the way you will learn tips and tricks about decluttering that will supplement your efforts.

Tips and Tricks

- Having a clean house doesn't mean you have an organized house. If your idea of cleaning is to throw everything under the bed, into the closet or into the garage then you really aren't being organized here

- Available space in the house is super important. Empty space not only looks nice, but it has a calming effect on your mind. Humans prefer wide open spaces to feeling cramped like a sardine. Just because some area of the house is empty doesn't mean that there is space there to put your electric fry cooker
- Some things take up more space than others. Large appliances and pieces of furniture make up the bulk of space usage. Be especially wary of buying new pieces of furniture or appliances if you know that space is an issue

Activity Section

1. The first step to solving a problem is understanding it. Figure out what your problem is in terms of your house. Write down somewhere what the major pain points are and which areas of the house need the most work. Document, on a scale from 1 to 10 how much work you think each room requires to be decluttered. Rank these from

highest to lowest. Now you have a basic list of priorities that need to be sorted.

2. Think about what needs you have relative to the free space in your house. What is free space in the first place? It is the balance between unused space and space that has some use. In other words, a closet has much free space but a corner of the room does not. More will be discussed about free space in later chapters.

   What are your needs in a purely commercial sense? You need food. For how many people? You need clothes. How often do you replace outfits? What do you do with the extra surplus? Think about the size of objects, the space they take up, and what value you ascribe to them. Do you really need that extra piece of furniture in the corner? Is your exercise machine being used as a clothes rack?

3. Do you consider yourself to be an organized person? Why or why not? If not, what changes would you have to make or how would your house have to look in order to change this consideration? And if you are an organized person, what are the issues that keep you from keeping the house in order? Think about the amount of free space available and the things that need to be

organized. Chances are, the problem isn't that you are disorganized, but that there simply isn't enough space for those things.

Chapter 2: One Step At A Time

Divide et impera – Latin Phrase

Rome was not built in one day and no war was won from a single battle. Following a formula is meant to be taken one step at a time. Say goodbye to spring cleaning once and for all, because after you find your ideal formula there will be no need for spring cleaning. The whole premise of it is fundamentally flawed. So called "deep cleaning" implies that something has gone neglected for a really long time and must be ousted like some malignant spirit that has taken residence within your floorboards.

These types of all-or-nothing cleaning attitudes make it easier to excuse bad behaviors. If you are going to dedicate an entire day (or week) to cleaning later in the year you might choose to "forget" to clean the carpet, or to throw a wrapper underneath the couch. Not only is this incredibly lazy, but it is also counterproductive. The more disorder you cause for yourself the more you will have to pay for it later.

The mind has its own way of seeing things. Basic senses like smell and sight are easily tricked. When was the last time you saw your nose without looking at a mirror? Its right under our eyes but our brain has learned to filter it out. The same happens with our familiar surroundings. A general mess is only unsightly until your brain gets used to it.

Has a guest ever said your house smelled a certain way and you were completely unaware? Maybe last night's shrimp dinner wasn't such a great idea. Covering odors with aerosol products and scented candles provide a temporarily solution. Stowing away junk inside of drawers and cupboards also only hides it from view. In reality it is still there.

And these objects in turn weigh down on your subconscious. Normally you won't notice them. But as soon as you open the closet or peer behind that cupboard you are immediately overwhelmed by the sight. This is what we are trying to avoid throughout this book. If you take the problem to its bare essentials and fight it step by step, you can succeed. This will take longer than going down the easy route but you will be rewarded handsomely in the end.

Divide and Conquer

Julius Caesar was well known for his ability to expand the size of Rome. Caesar knew that the best way to spread his influence over other kingdoms was to first break them down into smaller pieces. He did this by causing a division in their politics. Some were for him, others were against. Thus Caesar set out to create a shining image of Rome and offered rewards to anyone who joined. Smaller nations were broken up, with their people turned against each other. Roman Empire grew bigger while other nations grew smaller—ensuring that no nation could ever threaten it.

The problem at hand is difficult, and will never be solved by singular thinking. The problem needs to be broken down. But how? A naive approach may be to simply break down to individual rooms and to work on each room at a time. That would work, but it is a little short sighted. Rooms are independent of each other, and what you do in one room will not necessarily carry over to another room.

There is also the problem of upfront energy costs. Cleaning a house from top to bottom requires an immense amount of time and effort. This is why spring cleaning is traditionally done in the months of April and March. Or anytime past winter. Why? A possible explanation is that cold weather makes people lazy and they would rather wait for warmer temperatures. Another explanation could be that Spring coincides with the beginning of a new year and new beginnings. But Spring cleaning is probably just an arbitrary date.

Somewhere along the way you will be forced to make difficult decisions. Do I throw this thing out or do I keep it? Do I repair this or give it away? The average person will have a hard time making these decisions and can even be paralyzed by them as cognitive dissonance takes hold.

Dividing the problem into smaller steps addresses some of these concerns. You won't have to allocate high amounts of energy because now the problem is a fraction of what it used to be. Instead the problem is fixed through habit, and the continual use of those habits. The best habits are ones that are effortless, require very little mental energy and are effective at getting things done.

Our formula involves reversing the old habits that got the house cluttered in the first place. You replace the old with the new and the bad with the good. These changes are small, and will not be painful to make the switch. Nobody is saying you need to wake up tomorrow being a completely new you. You just have to make changes little by little.

How Do You Break Things Down?

The average college student knows at a very basic level that it is much easier to write an essay in two weeks than it is to write one over the weekend. Spread over a long period of time, the final product can be sliced into individual time slots. Research one day, write a little bit the next day and save a day or two for editing. Unfortunately, few students will follow a scheme like this. And that's a shame because there is power in the technique.

1. Eliminate Autopilot

Decluttering an extremely chaotic home may seem like a burdensome task at first. Where do you begin? How do you begin? How much time should you commit to the task? At the end of the day, a clean house will only get dirty over time, so these things shouldn't be stressed so much. What should be stressed however, is the way you make casual decisions. Too much of us go about our household affairs on "autopilot" mode. This is the tendency to do things haphazardly, not paying attention to the place and movement of objects around the house.

Autopilot mode is also responsible for many a soiled surface or fallen piece of trash that did not get picked up. We like to relax when we are in the home and that is perfectly okay. The key is to practice a sort of mindful relaxation, where you are still aware of your actions and what they cause to your home. Putting purpose behind your relaxation can help eliminate the mind's tendency to drift into autopilot.

On a macro scale you can try using a schedule or a predefined amount of time behind each activity. If you intend on watching TV, make sure you put an upper bound on that activity. If you promise to watch one more episode, make sure absolutely that it is only more episode. This primes your mind for disengaging from activities when it is time to be productive. The same technique can be extrapolated to other areas that might contribute to the mess in your home. This includes time spent on relaxation that could otherwise go towards tidying up.

Meanwhile on the micro scale, your actions need to reflect your intentions at all times. Remember that a house becomes disorderly overtime. The collection of all the actions taken within the household results in order or disorder. Every time a new item is added to your workspace, take note that it is there. Before the end of the day you should come up with some plan for that object. Otherwise it will stay there untouched.

When you read your mail, you should immediately know whether you will keep the document or throw it away. And if you do decide to keep it, make sure there is a predefined amount of time before you toss it in the trash. Otherwise useless mail will pile up.

These are but small examples of ways individual actions can matter.

2. Practice Seeing Small Problems Instead of Big Ones

A large problem like clearing out the mess in your house doesn't always present itself as smaller problems. At least not at first glance. All you know is that your house has an excess of things. Many of which don't know what to do with. There is a story behind every room in your house, and behind every single object that makes its way there. The key is to figure out what these stories are and to understand what they are trying to say.

Problem solving skills are synonymous with the break down of larger problems into smaller ones. A master problem solver is able to look at the "big picture" and to then find the smaller issues hidden within. Once these smaller problems are dealt with, everything else starts to fall into place.

So, the problems that concern your home probably have some list of smaller counterparts that are much easier to address. For example, a messy bathroom counter top can be fixed by sorting out small objects. You have makeup, creams, hair products, appliances, soaps and other miscellaneous items strewn in between. There is no space here, but an overabundance of options. Options, (especially superfluous ones) only tend to cause more stress than alleviate it.

The solution is to eliminate the options. Each object in that overcrowded bathroom is tackling a problem, but often they are not needed. Instead of saying I need all of these creams to address my bad skin, you can try using one or two products at a time, seeing what works, and then sticking with that. Everything else that is supplementary can be thrown out.

3. Substituting A Process For The Entire Whole

Trust in the process, not in the action. Hard work and consistency defeat talent. The old story of the tortoise and the hare reigns supreme time after time again. A routine is far superior than last minute attempts to clean the house. Never wait until the final moment, or find next week's dinner party as an excuse to finally wash the stove. These things should be done at regular intervals regardless of what comes next on the calendar.

A process or routine can help you maintain the appearance of your home over the long term. The beauty is that a routine doesn't have to amount to a high time investment. Simply moving one thing or quickly wiping a counter there after dinner can go a long way. Long term decluttering comes from these simple habits that you can do practically half asleep. A solid process is one that serves a purpose and that is easy to follow. A process can be as simple as throwing the trash out every X amount of days (even if the trash bag is not full yet). Another process can be throwing one thing out a day.

The process must match the needs of the household. If, for example, there is a regular influx of new things entering the house, there should be a process there to balance out the new with the old. People who regularly shop for each new season should be wary of the size of their wardrobe. Acquiring new clothes means that old clothes needs to be given away, repurposed, resold, or thrown out. This way you can build an internal alarm system. When you go to the mall to buy those new winter coats, a little alarm should be going off in your head that you need to figure out what to do with the old coats at home.

Processes should aim to keep the home in a perpetual balance. Over time you can decide how much of a thing you should allow, and how much of it needs to be removed.

4. Build A Conceptional Framework

When was the last time you examined something and looked at the small pieces that make up the whole? Everywhere you go you will see smaller things that make up larger ones. Things that fit like a puzzle piece to create a singular concept. Next time you are enjoying your favorite multigrain cereal see if you can identify the smallest constituents of the cereal and how they latch together. Are there fruits involved? How many unique pieces of cereal can you count? If you gently rumble your bowl (before pouring any milk) you can see how the pieces vibrate gently. Notice how some of the pieces prefer to go with others. The smaller ones get clumped together and separated from the larger ones. This is the basis for gravitational separation that is commonly used in industrial plants to sort things like recyclables.

Now when you look at your home try to see if you can find a conceptional framework at work. You walk in through the front door and what do you see? Note the time. If your home is like a system, it will have different inputs and outputs at different times. If you come late you might see that the dishes have yet to be put in the dishwasher, the living room has missing pillows, and so on. Clearly, the general area needs some straightening out to do.

You have just arrived home from work—and the house is neglected. Suppose you live with a spouse who is staying late at the office and you have two kids. The missing pillows in the living room was likely their doing. You can address the situation by stressing that your children need to return things to their usual spot. As you wind down from your return into the house (maybe change into comfortable clothes) you can throw the dishes into the dishwasher. That way you know that every time you come home from work you will have to repeat the process.

This is how a conceptual framework works. The small actions that you take to address it are like the small grains in your cereal. Tiny, but still part of the whole. Routines go hand in hand with building habits, and there is nothing wrong with them. A good routine takes a minimal amount of time, but can still make effective changes when they are followed over the days and months.

Tips and Tricks

- Don't be afraid to throw things out, even if they are perfectly good. Sometimes it is easier to get rid of something than do go through the trouble of re-purposing it. If there is some tension here, keeping old things for too long can lead to clutter.
- If you feel bad about throwing perfectly good things out, reconsider the next purchase you are making. If it still works fine, you probably don't need to make that purchase. In the long-run it very well may save you a great deal of stress
- There is a trade-off between donation and keeping your house in order. If you don't have a good enough system for making donations, then in the short term consider throwing things out instead
- Making a game out of something, or using the principles of "gamification" can vastly improve your attitude towards decluttering and especially the attitudes of young children. Make sure you have some reward system in place for following the rules. Every time you carry out a routine or process you should be able to reward yourself in some way.

- Yard sales are a great way of getting rid of things in the garage or extra clothes in the closet all while making a little bit of the money back

Activity Section

1. Think about your regular cleaning habits and how you schedule them. Once a week? Twice a week? What are the gamut of activities that usually follow? Are you one of those "spring cleaning" types? Pick just one of your cleaning routines and see if you can break it down into small chunks. Instead of doing this routine at regular intervals, try doing just a little bit everyday.
2. There is no right or wrong way to build a reward system—so long it rewards the long-term completion of goals. If you do not currently have one, take some time to consider the things that would motivate you to perform daily tasks. Maybe a big dinner out at your favorite restaurant? Or maybe a trip somewhere? The best kind of rewards are the ones that you work towards. Make sure to keep score on your progress.

Chapter 3: Opening Your Awareness

Watch your thoughts, they become words;
watch your words, they become actions;
watch your actions, they become habits;
watch your habits, they become character;
watch your character, for it becomes your destiny – Lao Tzu

The world is not a closed system. What you get from it depends on what you put back into it. Mindfulness started off as a movement aimed at slowing down. We spend too much of our days living inside of our heads, or behind some screen. When you become closed off from the rest of the world you make decisions that are less than ideal. Anxiety goes up, and you lose sight of the things that truly matter. For this reason mindfulness began with an emphasis on meditation and the practice of opening up awareness. Awareness y refers to the ability to take the world in, for what it is. Without judgment or any precognition. It is about experiencing the moment, for the moment.

You may ask what mindfulness and opening awareness has anything to do with decluttering the home. The answer is quite a lot, actually. Remember that Latin phrase from before: *Mens sana in corpore sano,* “a healthy mind inside a healthy body” and remember how we extended the phrase to also say, “a healthy mind inside a healthy body inside an orderly home”. Everything is connected, from the built environment to the tension that rises through your muscles and ultimately though the thoughts that consume your mind. Your thoughts then, are a reflection of the state of your home. But the same can be said of the reverse. The home and body could just as easily depend on your thoughts. The reverse means its possible to channel positive energy back down the chain through mindfulness.

Even if you don’t believe in things like positive energy and all that New Age mumbo jumbo that seems to be associated with meditation, you can still benefit from these principles. Mindfulness doesn’t have anything mystical or spiritual about it. All it does is give your mind a different way to interact with the world, thereby seeing beyond the daily anxieties that we may have. The end result is having a positive impact on your mood, your thoughts, your actions and ultimately on your habits. At the same time your relationship with others improves, as well as your relationship with your home.

How To Begin With Mindfulness

Meditation is not a requirement for mindfulness, but many do find it helpful. All you need is a quiet place that is free from distraction. Somewhere that is calm and that brings peace to your mind. Obviously, a messy house that is filled with objects will get in the way of this. Not only will it make meditation difficult, it will also make regular mindfulness a challenge. Your thoughts will be fixated on the state of the house, and in all the individual promises attached to different objects.

All that mindfulness requires is that you slow down your breath, your thinking, and that you allow yourself to simply feel. Turn off your thoughts even if just for a little bit. Allow yourself to sense things in a way that you never have before. Enjoy the silence. Enjoy the sounds of water running through the faucet or of a bird chirping outside your window. Even annoying sounds like the roar of a car engine can be enjoyable. They are just sounds entering your awareness. Close your eyes. Feel how your muscles relax with each breath and then stiffen. Just be in the moment.

If you perform this exercise a few times a day you will benefit from a general state of reduced anxiety. The exercise is designed to get you away from your troubles for a little bit. Remind yourself that there is a whole wide world out there that exists outside of your thoughts.

Now, mindfulness is all about bringing into your awareness the things that are happening at the present moment. This includes everything that your senses pick up. It also includes all the things that you are doing. The autopilot state of mind tends to takeover when your mind is full of anxious thoughts. Why? Because as humans we do not like experiencing unpleasant things. Instead we seek things that are easy and quick to release some form of pleasure. If our mind thinks it is easier to buy a new gadget than to address the clutter problem, then it will buy the new gadget.

Mindfulness is the complete opposite of anxiety. When you open up your awareness you are validating every single feeling that exists. If something is hard, you pay attention to it. You no longer live inside your head and you are able to make the correct decisions. You are able to give greater care to your surroundings.

How to Apply Mindfulness To The Home

The practice of mindfulness teaches us many things. For one, it teaches us to ease up a little bit. Nothing can be so serious as the quiet pleasure of existing itself. Everyday is a gift, every single action that you take is like a fresh breath of air. The best thing to do is take what mindfulness has taught you and begin to use it in the context of decluttering your home. Nothing is too precious that you can't do away with. Physical objects are just things—most of them can be replaced without incident. What is truly precious are the tomorrows that we are given and the way that we spend them.

A messy home is like an assault on the senses. Objects stacked up to the ceiling are an eyesore. The lack of negative space inside the house makes us feel like we are trapped. Counters become congested with appliances and other things. The halls are lined with stowed away boxes and pieces of furniture that make it difficult to walk. Sometimes the house looks like a work in progress more than a house. Like if we just moved in a few weeks ago and are still getting settled. Sometimes a move can take months or years for everything to find a place of belonging.

Mindfulness allows us to see beyond all of this. There is no judgment when you bring these things into awareness. But for the sake of having an organized home, there has to be at least some sense of judgment. You have to fill that gap and graciously decide when something needs to be put away. Eyesores are easy to identify. They simply feel out of place.

The aim is to put an end to the disorganization. Limit the amount of disorganization inside the home by limiting what you bring in, and being mindful about how objects are placed within. One way to look at it is imagining a young child who likes to eat. One day the family goes out to an all you can eat buffet. The grownups know that just because it is all you can eat, you should still pace yourself. You could say that the grownups possess some mindful awareness that the child lacks. Instead the child eats and eats, without paying attention to what or why. In the end the poor child gets a bad stomach ache.

1. Using The Awareness of Others

The people that surround us in our life are very important. Being aware of what others are feeling is a trait that goes hand in hand with mindfulness. Empathy, sometimes called emotional intelligence, is a facet of mindfulness because you are tuning in to the lives of others. You are acting as a conduit for all the emotions of people in the general vicinity.

Someone with good people skills is able to read the "mood" of a room and knows how to navigate it. Certain situations have different moods. Something that is appropriate in one instance may be out of line in another. There is nothing particularly special about knowing how to do this. A great deal of our communication happens without even saying a word. Close to 90% of all human communication is nonverbal. These are the body language cues, the expressions and gestures that hint what a person may be feeling.

You might be astounded by what you can uncover by tuning in your awareness to those who are around you. You can pick up little ticks that a person may have, or how they tend to carry themselves when they are out of the spotlight. These things are important for gauging what the other person is feeling.

Much can be accomplished by simply putting yourself in the shoes of others. And this is particularly relevant to planning out your home because you won't be the only one using it. Think about how your family or spouse feels about the things and the organization of the home. Would they prefer to have a house that is kept or one that is all over the place? Think about the needs of the many vs the needs of the few (yourself).

And those who live alone will still have the inevitability of having a guest over. Even those people can use mindfulness to spruce up their living arrangements. Most people for example, prefer to be able to make out the walls of their house or apartment. Mindfulness in that sense is less about reading peoples needs and more about conformity. Not that there is anything wrong with conformity.

Think about what the significance of clutter is from the basis of society. For most, clutter hurts to look at. It doesn't really belong in the house. Think about all the things you do in private, and how many of those behaviors you would be appalled if someone saw you do them in public. The idea of mindfulness through awareness of others follows the same principles. Not to make you feel paranoid that somebody may be watching, but to make you cognizant of the everyday decisions that you are making.

If, for example, you have so much kitchenware that your cups no longer fit in the cupboards you may consider getting rid of some. Any child who happened to come in the house would immediately point these things out to you. They are things that are obvious to others but hidden to us.

2. Being Mindful of the Possessions Cycle

The possessions cycle refers to the cyclical nature in which things are acquired, disposed of and renewed. Everyone has some form of trash accumulation in their homes. Trash pickup is a vital part of society. The city or local municipality is often tasked with collecting everyone's garbage. If this didn't happen, everyone would be buried in trash.

Things don't last forever. Not even our biggest monuments or core infrastructure would last for more than a few hundred years if it wasn't being constantly replaced. Our modern economy is based on products that are designed to fail after a certain amount of use. New smartphones come out everyday. There always seems to be some new "smart" gadget that has hit the market, each having the potential to take up valuable space inside of your home.

But it's not just space that they take away from you. It's also your sanity and sense of freedom that is being worked on. Things—whatever they may be—imply some sort of utility or use case. That is, they beg for some type of human action. Your brain knows this, and reacts negatively when given too many options to use. Or when you try to perform some task and some of your clutter is getting in the way of that.

Like the hungry child in the all you can eat buffet, many of us go through the possessions cycle without being mindful of our appetites. And just like the child, we can get sick from it. Though for us it's not the stomach ache that we suffer from, but the anxiety and feelings of being overwhelmed within our own house. This is a terrible feeling that shouldn't be felt by anyone.

How do we get out? One simple solution is to simply buy less things. But buying isn't the only way we get stuff. Sometimes we are gifted things. Other times we come across something and simply decide to pick it up. Overwhelmingly though, we acquire things by using our wallets. Most of these things we don't really need. Since humans are materialistic something inside us compels us to collect, pick up and save things for later.

Some of this may be a leftover survival mechanism from our distant past. Back then it did make sense to hoard things (usually food) to make it through times of scarcity. But the human race left scarcity behind many thousands of years ago. There really isn't any reason to stock up on things, especially in the developed world.

Pleasure shoppers are the most at risk group for falling victim to the possessions cycle. But they aren't the only ones. Anyone who has a tendency to hold on to things is also at risk. Unfortunately, much of this has to do with past traumas about loss. Mindfulness can help. There is a split decision between the time it takes to acquire an object and then bring it home to join your other things.

A good protocol for the possessions cycle is asking yourself a few questions. First, ask yourself what you need. Are there things in the house that need to be repaired or replaced? Or is there some other area that is simply missing? If so, then consider buying X products to make up the need. And here is where the mindfulness step kicks in. Now that this other product has been acquired, it is time to factor it in with the rest.

The preferred order of priority here is to first repair, then replace, and finally to get something new (if all other options are exhausted). Not here that getting something new doesn't imply buying something that is *new*. It can be a secondhand object, like a used car. So long as it performs all the utility that you need from it that a brand new version would.

First repair. This involves identifying a need that is not being met, or a need that was met sometime in the past and has stopped being fulfilled because of malfunction. If at all possible, (and if cheaper than replacing the object) then get it fixed.

Next, replace the object if repairing it isn't feasible. Note here that replacing means getting rid of the old thing. And this is the crucial step. The old product *must* be replaced sooner or later. Of course, sooner is always better than later. Because then we forget or get lazy and it just becomes another entry on our errand list.

Ideally, something that has been replaced should be out of the house within the first week of receiving the new version. Certainly this should take no more than one month. That should give you plenty of time (if you are mindful of your time) to get rid of the old thing. Sell, donate or simply throw out if the first two are unavailable.

3. Taking Mindfulness Into Your Own Hands

Mindfulness is tricky for many people because they feel like they lack direction. It is one thing to explain how to practice mindfulness and another thing to implement it. In the context of ridding the home of clutter, mindfulness can be taken up a notch by following simple routines and exercises.

For example, visualizing how to use awareness of others can be difficult when living alone. The good thing is that you are never quite alone—you still have yourself. And this can work to your benefit if you observe your own attitude towards your home and the things inside of it. You can achieve this by forming a regular habit of journaling.

The journal need not be special. Just a few notes in a book or smartphone app will suffice. You want to record what the state of your house is (or if you have a few problem areas that you want to focus on). You should write down anytime you feel overwhelmed by the clutter, and why. What was the action you where trying to achieve and found difficult? Why was it difficult? And make sure to write down what the severity of the clutter was. A scale from 1 through 10 works well.

Then, the next time you feel yourself getting anxious or upset because of the clutter, you can revisit your notes and see what you have written about it in the past. Note what the severity of the clutter was, and if it got better or worse over time. The journal in conjunction with regular cleaning and reorganization efforts can work wonders. Over time you may identify certain objects or groups of objects that give you problems. And over time you will think about solutions about how to deal with them. The purpose of the journal is the record improvements.

Those who balk at the idea of writing can also take photos with their smartphone. The same principle applies. Take photos of a room or area of the house over time, and see how the clutter piles up or how it slims down. Identify what your trouble points are.

What seems to stay over days, weeks and months? What about this thing is so important that you simply can't get rid of? And is it a problem?

The photo method also allows you to tap into the awareness of others albeit indirectly. You can imagine that these photos will be going up on a social media post (you don't actually have to post them), and then explore how they make you feel. Would you be comfortable showing those pictures to the rest of the world? To your parents? To potential romantic partners?

4. Mindfulness of Need And Obsession

It is easy to say that something is needed when there is an obvious lack of that something. It's just as easy to say that something isn't needed when there is an abundance of that thing. This is central to the pack rat's dilemma, where every object seemingly has a purpose and can be used for later. The problem here is clear as day. Ordinary objects, or things that come in duplicates are suddenly just as important as filling the need that is unmet.

This is dangerous thinking in the world of two for one deals, mega value packs and other marketing dribble designed to sell products. Products can very quickly pile up if someone lacks the mindfulness of their shopping habits. And then the question becomes, even if I do have this need, how much of it needs to be filled before I can say that I am satisfied?

There is a fine line here between need and obsession. Obsession is anything that goes on masquerading as a need when it has probably already been met. For example, somebody who wants a better sounding TV might decide they need a sound system. This is a luxury, but if the budget allows it, its a perfectly valid need a person might feel. Getting the sound system installed should fulfill this need. But when this person starts to buy additional speakers and sound systems for other rooms, we may say that it is an obsession.

The tricky part is that an obsession isn't necessarily bad. Maybe this person simply loves music, and must absolutely have the best quality sound systems. There is no issue with that. That problem arises if and when an obsession grows to the point where other areas of the house start to suffer. Most notably, when negative space starts to be eaten up by these "extra" things that serve a small purpose.

A hungry person has a tremendous need for eating food. We've all been there, getting off from work and all too eager to get a quick bite at the fast food joint. As soon as our teeth dig into that juicy burger our need for food starts to go down. Our filled meter goes up, and eventually we are satisfied. That first burger that you eat has immense utility. It is very valuable to you because it gave you energy. Now imagine what if you got two burgers instead, or three or four. Each additional burger that you eat feels a little not so great. It might bring you pleasure. It might bring you utility. But it will never compare to the first burger that you ate, which made you feel happy and no longer hungry.

In economics we call this the marginal utility of a product. Once a person owns at least one of the things, they receive less use from buying additional units. People who show signs of obsession either choose to ignore the marginal utility of objects, or they neglect to think about the consequences of their obsession.

This is where mindfulness can again help. Mindfulness is what tells you that there is a problem when for example, eating that second burger. Your mind tells you that you probably shouldn't have another. Yet some people who are addicted to eating fast food will not catch the hopelessness of marginal utility. What most people fail to realize is that marginal utility will always come at a cost. Money and time sure, but also space, freedom, and opportunities if we are talking about clutter in the home.

It is important that you are able to tell the difference between need, utility and obsession when you are making purchases. Doing so will limit the amount of junk that you retain in the home.

Tips and Tricks

- A simple yet effective way to increase your mindfulness is to practice meditation daily
- Explore different ways that you can meditate. If you are so inclined, join a class
- Remember that mindfulness is less an emotional state and more akin to a lifelong practice
- Mindfulness teaches us to be wary of others around us. Besides being aware of their emotional state, remember to always be kind and accommodating towards those we care about. This includes not making any mess in other peoples homes and taking care of our own living space
- In conjunction with meditation you can also try Yoga as a relaxation technique
- The connection between mind, body and built environment is most obvious when talking

about self improvement. If we are good to our bodies then we get regular exercise, plenty of sleep and adequate nutrition. Likewise, being good to the home should come with its own set of practices that create harmony

- In many cultures around the world it is customary to remove footwear before entering past the threshold of the home. This is a form of mindfulness both on the part of visitors and of the hosts. That way dirt and grime doesn't get into the home, and at the same time they are showing respect for the home

Activity Section

1. Those who are having a hard time getting into the mindfulness mindset can use a few "affirmations" meant to be repeated inside the head or aloud. An affirmation is positive in nature, repetitive, and designed to motivate. Examples may include "I am here. I am free. This is my home and I take care of it", "Today there are many opportunities to improve. Let me see these opportunities and make actions based of them", "Things are

nice, but I don't need them all. To be good to myself I should use less things".

Try to get into the habit of using some positive affirmations throughout the day, or when you are feeling overwhelmed. Create new affirmations depending on how you feel.

2. Use both the journal technique and the smartphone camera technique over a period of one week. Examine how you feel during each day and think about what changes you can make to feel better, both about yourself and about the state of the home. If you don't see any good results after one week, try going for another. In six months from now you should see a big difference.

   Using a week is a good general time frame because you are more likely to log in the journal everyday. Over time you might forget to do these things and the technique doesn't work as well. It requires regular updates.

3. Take a quick inventory of any purchases you plan on making in the following month (not including groceries). What needs are you intending to fulfill by making those purchases? If you can't think about any and still plan on making a purchase then there is a

problem. Ask yourself if that problem is part of a deeper obsession.

If you can't find a need that you plan on correcting with a purchase, go through the protocol discussed earlier in this chapter. First see if there is some object that needs to be repaired, replaced, or if buying a different product is preferable.

4. Look around you. What are some of the eyesores that stick out most to you? For each of those items, follow the same protocol in reverse. Try to figure out what need those things are supposed to fill. Notice where you have duplicates. Nothing is wrong with having more of one of a thing (having extra rolls of toilet paper for example). But sometimes duplicates contribute to the clutter in the house. More about duplicates is covered in Chapter Four.

   If you can't figure out what need an object is fulfilling, then perhaps it is time to say goodbye to it. Next, see if you can identify those pesky objects that you have already replaced with a different object and are just laying around the house. Remember that when you replace something the ideal time frame for getting rid of the old version is one month. After that these things just pile up. See if you can find any items that you can immediately toss out.

Chapter 4: Identifying The Organizational Deficit

Organization goes a little deeper than simply putting like things together (though that in itself is a good start). We all know that whites go with whites, darks with darks, and colors with colors. Most of us can at least appreciate that books on the shelf should go in alphabetic order by authors name. That much is the easy kind of organization. It will only take you so far towards clearing out your living space.

The type of organization you are looking for is the kind that sorts out priorities throughout each room. People who know what they want in life and how they want to structure their lives tend to have neat homes. What more is a home than a collection of personal possessions? Each possession should have some form of purpose or utility for that household. If not, then why is that object in the house? An object that does not have a purpose doesn't belong.

Furthermore, each household presents a series of trade-offs. Should the house be large or small? How much does the house cost? What are the construction materials? How many rooms, amenities and different layouts are available? The configurations of the home will present their own sets of issues. The matter in which you organize your possessions throughout different rooms highly depend on the configuration.

Do you pick large, imposing furniture or do you go with a minimalist look? Are your walls bare or do you adorn them with posters and other trinkets? What sort of appliances do you need in the house? The answers to these questions are more important than you think. Because they tell you what you want out of your living space. If you know the answers, you can make better choices about the clutter that you collect. If you don't know the answers, then ask yourself what your current and future needs are.

Home As a Reflection Of Personal Values

They say to never judge a book by its cover, but what about judging a person by their contents of the house? Here the word "judge" is perhaps too strong a word. If you were to look inside the private residence of the average person, you can often tell a fair bit about them purely by the contents. You can guess at their careers, hobbies, and size of their family rather quickly. You can also sometimes tell what their religious and cultural background are simply be observing the type objects that they have.

You can also tell how well that person is organized. If everything looks neat and orderly, you know that they pay attention to their allocation of resources. They are probably efficient people who take pride in the appearance of their humble abode. Then when you see the trashy living area of the average bachelor pad or college student dorm and you get an idea of what kind of person they are as well. They are probably dealing from a mishmash of priorities, having to juggle a social life with part-time work and studying. Or maybe they just like to party and not clean up after themselves. Young people seem to care less about their living arrangements since they move often.

When the home is in perfectly harmony with personal values and goals the clutter is suddenly gone. You only keep what you need to live the way you want to. But your priorities need not be set in stone. People tend to be fluid beings with changing aspirations. However, having a solid base of these priorities certainly helps keep things organized.

Other times it seems like the home is a reflection of the character of the person who lives there. We like to think that a CEO will have a perfectly thought out home. Everything is where it needs to be and everything is clean. Unlike the average person the CEO can afford to hire a maid, or an entire army of maids to clean their homes. The average person's home more directly reflects on what kind of person they are, but not exclusively.

Clutter just happens. During the worst of times and during the best of times, things around the house just seem to appear. It is how the person decides to deal with clutter that is the defining feature that matters. The two general attitudes towards for dealing with it. Either you throw everything away. Or you decide to squeeze things in.

Outside observers will feel like clutter in your home is a bad judge of character because clutter is messy. Nobody wants to see what they think is your personal trash pile. They may think you are lazy or that you don't care about having a messy looking home. But what they don't know is that the clutter is just temporary problem you are dealing with. Don't feel that clutter is part of you. It certainly doesn't have to be. Clutter is just there. Like the dust that accumulates on the windowsill over time.

Part of accepting the inevitability of clutter has to do with accepting things for what they are. It is incredibly liberating to accept that clutter has become part of your life. This is the same as being mindful of where you are. You are here, right here and right now. Whatever surrounds you is also part of the now. Understand and acknowledge it. But also know that you are the master of yourself, and that you can make the necessary changes. If it begins to rain on you, then simply move towards some shelter.

Knowing that there is a problem is the first step. The next step is to identify what the weak points are that lead to that problem. Leave behind this idea that clutter comes from within. Or that there is something inherently wrong with you. Clutter manifests itself naturally, from the complex interactions of the market and to your unique needs. Your job is to develop the healthy habits that allow you to deal with clutter and not be drowned in it.

What Is An Organizational Deficit?

Something is probably lacking in your life, and it certainly isn't the clutter. It could be a lack of self-reflection in your daily movements, but it could also have to do with the way your mind works. Or more specifically, with the things that your mind are focused on. Usually we don't pay attention to things like the organization of the household unless we are just barely moving in. After that, our attention drifts into other equally important areas in our lives. The maintenance left up to no one. We just assume that things will find their way to their proper place over time. But this is a false hope. You should never expect things to work out on their own.

The results of careless, automatic actions usually leads to disorder. The opposite is having a well grounded organizational foundation from which you base decisions off of. Organization doesn't have to be a long drawn out concept like design. All you need to get started is patience and the ability to be mindful of your space.

The Law of Categories

Everywhere around you there are categories. Any object that is a noun can be categorized into some class. So can numbers. Categories have a niche spot in philosophical thinking but they also play a role in the organization of your home. You clutter can be divided into categories and subcategories to help you decide what to do with it.

It's not correct to say that everything in your house is useful when so much of it comes off as junk. Neither is it right to say that all clutter is trash. Both of these things are symptoms of an organizational deficit within your way of thinking. For example, any collection of things in your house may be cumbersome at face value, but they can be extremely useful to people who are in need. When getting rid of these things it's better to donate than to throw away. At the same time, saying that you *must* hold on to anything because you might need it in the future doesn't make sense. Perhaps you may need it sometime down the road, but is it really worth having it in the short term? What if it was contributing to disorder in the house?

The issue at the heart of all this is marginal utility mentioned in the previous chapter. It's not possible for everything to be useful, nor is it possible for everything to be equally useless. There is a balance in between the two, and it depends on what your needs are. The law of categories says that any object has an affinity for similar ones, and that their utilities are dependent on each other.

Categories of things can be broken down into like objects and objects that fulfill similar needs. Food, vegetables, fruits, meats, instant dinners and so on are all groceries. They serve an obvious role. Books, magazines, and newspapers serve a different role, to inform. Together they make up a whole, which is a singular need you may have.

When thinking about collections of things, do not feel overwhelmed. Nor should you feel like you must keep everything. Instead think in terms of categories of things.

Understanding Negative Space

Negative space is anywhere that you can look and see nothing in particular. If your house was a canvas or web page, the negative space is the same as the blank white space that makes up the margins. Nothing is supposed to go there, but it serves a distinct purpose. In print media white space is used to enhance user experience and to make the letters more legible.

When it comes to your house, negative space or empty space plays the role of creating harmony. Small children who neglect to clean their rooms often come out into the living room or kitchen (where it is much more neater) to play with their toys. Since their rooms have become too cluttered to get around, they look to other rooms that have more empty space. The same principle is at play when you go to a crowded social event and you look for some fresh air to get away from it all.

As humans we do not like cramped spaces (with a few exceptions). Negative space helps to calm down our nerves after a long day sitting at work and then battling our ways through traffic. Negative space is like a soft blanket that allows our minds to simmer down and to wander about. Think about your bathroom and how our minds like to wader while taking a shower. The shower is perhaps the least cluttered area in any house, because we bathe there. It is incumbent on us to keep this area as clear as possible. We don't want to accidentally trip on something.

The rest of the house doesn't get this same treatment as much as it should. Instead we see empty space as an opportunity to add more and more junk. Space is important; houses are not storage units that you can stuff with a random assortment of things before its filled to the brim. Instead the collections you find inside must be carefully considered to both fit your needs and to maintain the harmony throughout.

If you consider that space is one of your needs just like eating and drinking are, then you might have a different attitude towards how you organize your things. Halls should be empty of clutter. Adorned walls are fine, by physical objects that impede traffic through space are a big no-no.

Other areas to be wary of empty space include the kitchen and living area, and especially in the bedroom. Sleeping is one of the most important bodily functions we have, and a crowded room does not invite sleep easily. Instead it invites anxious thoughts and a sense of overcrowding.

What About Duplicates?

Duplicates can be difficult from an organizational standpoint. On the one hand, duplicates can make up clear instances of a category and not be bothersome. On the other, duplicates can eat up available space and make your life a nightmare. As with most things the solution is to maintain a balance between the two extremes. Nobody bats an eye if a family of five own two or three cars. But once that number rises and cars start appearing parked in the sidewalk then it may become an issue.

A duplicate of a thing has clear intrinsic value. If one thing is valuable then having more of the thing should also retain some of that value. This is especially true with perishable goods. If you know something won't last for long, it may be helpful to keep extras at hand. But this creates the dilemma of availability and storage. In any major city you can find just about any household item in a store. One doesn't need to go more than a few miles to find it. Buying that twenty four mega pack might be a great deal, but then you have to factor in the size constraint. Where do you keep it? Will you have to give up some negative space to store it?

Duplicates are not really needed. Most of them come into the home because we are lazy and would rather not make extra trips to the store. When a certain need is fulfilled by one or a few, there is no rush to then go and buy more. Even if they are on sale.

Something that you know will last for a long time has less justification owning more than one. You wouldn't buy two big screen TV's, for example. And yet people still come to possess two of something when they already have the one. Kitchen appliances are notorious offenders. People buy a pressure cooker, a slow cooker, an air fryer, waffle maker, and the list goes on and on. In most cases the slow cooker and the pressure cooker are interchangeable. A waffle maker is a luxury, and so is the air fryer to a degree. These aren't direct duplicates per say, but they play the same role.

These appliances will take up space on your counter tops and walk ways. Most of them will not fit inside your drawers (unless you have many). All of these products belong in the same category more or less, which is food and kitchen related. A college student living on their own for the first time has more reason to purchase a pressure cooker than a stay at home mom who already has a well established kitchen. They are by no means the required way to prepare food.

The bottom line is that duplicates are big empty space eaters. Duplicates that belong to the same categories should be severely limited. Avoid splurging on combo pack deals if you know what space will be an issue.

Tips and Tricks

- Negative space should come at a premium in your home. Bringing new things into the house should factor for it, not just the cost of the product
- Categories may refer to objects that fulfill the same needs. They can also refer to objects that logically go together, like books in the same bookcase, hygiene products in the bathroom and so on
- No one category should be larger than any other category in terms of taking up space. Categories that have many sub categories and overlap into others may be larger
- A duplicate within a category is a clear indication that a need has already been fulfilled. At that point, you should stop increasing the quantity within that category
- If you sense that negative space inside the home is running out, the next solution is to get rid of objects or to move them to traditionally confined spaces like attics and closets
- Sticking everything out of sight is not the ideal solution, but it is still preferable to

cluttering up your previous negative space. Once you can longer avoid filling up negative space it is time to start getting rid of things

- A good rule of thumb for dealing with duplicates is as follows. If the product isn't long lasting, keep enough extra to last a week. If the product isn't long lasting and you have more than one, either move that object into storage or get rid of it. Remember that you can always go and buy new things when they run out. Money doesn't take up space

Activity Section

1. Try to think about what categories are in your household. Which ones do you regularly use, which ones are only used on occasion, and which ones almost never. Remember that a category can be any broad topic of objects. A category can also be all of the different objects that fulfill a specific need. Beauty products can be one category of like things. You TV, stereo, laptop, and gaming console can be a category of items you use for entertainment.

   There is no right or wrong answer to figure

out what these categories may be. Make a game out of it and see how many different categories you can identify. Then when you can't think about any more, put the list somewhere highly visible like on a fridge. In the following days see if you can find any additional categories that pop into your head.

2. Identify what the top three categories are in your household that contribute the most to your clutter. Avoid picking the pick things simply because they take up large amounts of negative space. Things like the fridge, stove, beds, and other pieces of furniture have a greater priority than miscellaneous items. If you do feel that furniture takes up too much space then identify which pieces cause the most pain.

   Within those top three categories, begin to identify which individual items cause the most problems. Make an effort to get rid of these things. If you can't throw them away, begin making a plan for donating or selling them.

   Remember what these categories are. They will follow you every time you make purchasing decisions.

3. Pick one room that has a lack of negative space compared to the others. Make this your

new long term project room. The goal is to get rid of excess items. Sometimes rooms are so cluttered we can't see the floor anymore. Or parts of the wall. Try to fix this.

Chapter 5: Saying No to Inaction

Passion first and everything will fall into place. – Holly Holm

If each object found in the home is treated as a promise to do something in the future, then inaction results in a backlog of possible actions. This is evident when someone neglects to use something they own. Over time the thing, whatever it may be, begins to gather dust. Meanwhile new items enter the home and old items are hardly ever discarded. We forget they are even there until one day you bump into them. When they come into awareness it is very likely that we acknowledge we haven't used them in a long time. Maybe not since we first got them.

This makes us uneasy, because we know there is some future where we should someday find a use for it. After all we paid money for that item. But since we are busy and because we don't have a current reason to use that item, we leave it for another day. You are making a promise that you will use that object eventually. But what is the probability of that happening?

Promises are difficult to keep when our lives change so frequently. Since change is always a constant throughout life, old promises are likely to be broken. This true both from the relationship perspective and from the perspective of making goals. At the turn of the new year we might purchase gym memberships and workout equipment. Others will decide to take up a new hobby, and lug hobby related things like paints, easels, wood for carving, musical instruments and so on into the house. Then as we get back into our daily routines these objects are quickly forgotten. Part of this is a failure of goal setting and part of it is a failure of making too many promises.

Remember that humans have infinite desires but limited space. They also have a limited amount of time. Only twenty four hours a day in fact. A majority of that time is either spent working, sleeping or at school. What little leisure time that is left gets split in-between chores, family obligations and relaxation. It is far too easy to underestimate the time commitment that an object requires relative to the amount of space they occupy.

Take the computer for an example. Compared to the rest of your things a computer is hardly a burden. Stick it on your desk inside a corner somewhere and forget about it. Small that it may be, a computer can take up a disproportionate amount of time commitment. The same goes with your TV or any other electronic device. Someone could spend hours upon hours in front of these possessions, all without contributing to negative space in the house.

This feature is hardly found in other objects you may have. Scattered objects with no clear use cases are more likely to pile up and contribute the most to negative space. These are your problem cases. You don't want to throw them away but you also don't want to use them. At least not yet.

Clutter then, is inherently linked to indecisiveness. The inability to make decisions is worsened by the overwhelming feeling of being surrounding by objects of questionable value. Each one is like a burden on your decision making potential. There are more mental calculations you need to make if you have more objects lying around. These are more promises that you have to make to yourself.

Though you may not realize it, a failure to make a decision is still a type of decision. The inability to take action is still creating some form of activity on your part (the lack of any action). This might be difficult to grasp, but know that there is no such thing as inactivity from a decision making point of view. Everything you decide to do (or don't) is still having an effect on your life.

Your home is no exception. When you fail to make use of something, or to get rid of it, those decisions contribute to the overall accumulation of objects. The issue can be traced back to a failure to categorize something and at the same time gauge its value to you. An object that is hardly used may fall into a logical category with the rest of your possessions but this is like an empty concept. In math we say it is an empty set.

These objects are not being used anymore. They belong to another category, one of the disused items. In the majority of cases, this category needs to be kept to an absolute minimum to maintain harmony throughout the household. When this category grows too large, it starts to eat into the other categories that your possessions belong to. Before long, the category of disused items is the largest compared to the others. And this is a huge problem.

The Terrible Three

There are three main culprits that prevent people from keeping the disuse category small. The first is the inability to make actions which we have already covered. Second there is procrastination, which prolongs the time required to take action. And lastly, that there is a lack of time for making these decisions. At the end of the day everyone will have to face them. It is better to acknowledge that these things exist sooner rather than later. Doing so will tell you where you are, and what steps you might need to take to fix them. Ignoring them will be like ignoring the problem, and that never results in meaningful solutions.

1. Addressing The Inability to Make Decisions

Organizational debt will have to be repaid eventually. Oftentimes with interest. A house that already has a high organizational debt needs to be sorted out before any major revisions are made. Any future purchases should be put on hold while you figure out what to do with the old stuff. The mantra of repair, replace and buying new can help with some of this debt but not all of it. Once you have repaired everything that needs fixing, you are still left at the same place. Even if you replace things by throwing out the old, the balance of objects remains the same (which is good, but still not enough). And if you buy new objects to fulfill the needs that old objects where satisfying, you must decide what to do with the old ones.

In essence, you have to slim down and get rid of things. But since you are decisive this is incredibly hard to do. We cringe at the idea of throwing out things that at one point costed us money. Or things that have some humanitarian value like food, clothes, and bedding. You must accept that throwing things out is sometimes the only solution. Not everything can be donated or sold. Even so you certainly should try to exhaust those options before leaving everything to the landfill.

If donating or selling objects is too much of a hassle there is no shame in simply throwing them out. On the one hand somebody else could of used those products but on the other, you are freed from the organizational debt that these objects incur. The trade off doesn't seem so bad if you are still creating a net positive in your life. Doing good in one area tends to spread that positivity around. If you become a less anxious, more organized person by throwing out things then the entire world is still benefiting from that. Visitors to your home benefit, and every member of the household also benefits. Your every relationship is suddenly enhanced because you got rid of things that were having a negative impact on your life.

We also tend to keep objects of sentimental value. Just about everyone has some box in the attic or shed filled with old mementos from when they were younger. Or things passed down from generations or souvenirs from vacations. Besides having infinite wants, humans also have an infinite capacity and interest for feeling nostalgia. Which in itself isn't bad, so long as there is balance everywhere else. Most people can afford to keep a box stashed away somewhere without giving up too much negative space. Mementos don't really have a use besides for nostalgia. Since you want these things to last, they won't get any mileage.

Objects of sentimental value may take a pass, but not *all* objects will. In other words, not every object you own has sentimental value. And if they do, it is a sign something is wrong. It's possible that you confuse your inability to throw things out with sentimental attachment. Just because something has been hanging around a long time doesn't mean it has intrinsic value to you. It just feels that way. Our brains simply think that if something has always been a certain way that things ought to stay that way. And herein lies the issue with decision making. Nothing gets thrown out. Nothing gets done.

If the clutter around you is due to difficulty making decisions there are a few solutions you might consider. The simplest of which simply means grabbing a trash bag and stuffing as many objects in there that get in your way. Then just throw it out. Don't stuff it in a corner. Don't even think about it. Just do it. Usually we overthink what we ought to do, then we second guess ourselves and suddenly we have thought up one hundred reasons why we should keep things instead. Thinking is often the enemy if you are trying to declutter. Free yourself from thinking.

2. Addressing Procrastination

Procrastination occurs when we put things off for later. There is a clear correlation between procrastination and the accumulation of things in the house. If decision making is difficult or unpleasant, we would rather do something else. Then we quickly forget that there was a decision to be made in the first place. This is bad for obvious reasons, but you may not realize that you are doing this. First, the home is usually regarded as a place for relaxation. We know that we should keep things clean enough so that we are comfortable and free of sickness. We clean after pets, wipe surfaces from bacteria and make sure we can walk around without impediment.

Not enough emphasis is put on negative space and the possible sicknesses that come from feeling cramped. Truly these are sicknesses. It is not normal for someone to feel overwhelmed in the confines of their own home. It is not normal for someone to feel anxious simply because they want to go into the kitchen and make a sandwich. You shouldn't dread having to walk through the front door of your own home.

What if you have no issue with making decisions, but find yourself putting those decisions off for later? Or maybe you feel like it is okay to prolong the decisions because something might happen in the future that changes your mind about an object? These are still largely symptoms of being a procrastinator. The issues you are dealing with are not in the future, though you might like to think that they are. Clutter is a very immediate problem, one that should be fixed as soon as possible.

The clutter then becomes an issue of self-discipline. You need to force yourself to organize the house. You need to make a deliberate inquiry about the objects that are in your house. Know what you have, why you have it, and whether it is of any use. Thing's that have not been used in a while and that have little current use should probably be removed from the house. There is no need to have two objects that fulfill the same purpose.

And if by chance you are stocking up on food and fuel for the coming nuclear apocalypse, you probably don't need to. The chances of stockpiles ever being required are so slim that it doesn't make sense to put yourself under that kind of stress. The longest time frame any food should be stored in the pantry is at most, six months. Food shouldn't be frozen for much longer than that, either.

Defeating procrastination requires a mindful understanding that you will use deliberate action. It requires that you are able to identify those instances when you begin to procrastinate and then be able to correct them. To catch yourself in the act as it were. This shouldn't be too hard if you are already making it a habit to use mindfulness every time you use things around the house.

There is a connection between visual acuity and the urge to do something easier. Its pretty easy to tell when the house's negative space becomes inundated with stuff. But since its easier to simply look away at something more appealing like a screen the impulse to do something about it goes away. An aggressive scheduling system or to-do list can help face these feelings. If you make it a habit to regularly get rid of a few things every now and then, procrastination becomes less of an issue.

See that motivation comes and goes. You shouldn't pay too much attention to it because one day it is there and the next day it is gone. What you need instead is repetition. Through repetition you can create your own motivation. Throw a few things out and see what difference it makes.

3. Addressing a Lack of Time

What if you neither lack the ability to make decisions nor do you fall victim to procrastination? There is still at least one possible reason why clutter exists in your house, and that is simply that you don't have to time to do something about it. Time availability is usually related to procrastination. It could very well be that you have the time, your willingness just isn't there. So which one is it?

One can always make time by giving up non-essential commitments like pleasure and relaxation. Even people who say they don't have time for these things can make it work around their schedules. If you consider the task of decluttering the home reasonably similar to reading a book, the task can be finished over a long period of time. Maybe you don't have the time to completely reorganize your home and find which objects you still need and which are bunk. Fine. But do you have the time to organize the cereal boxes on your fridge? Or to do something about the random toolbox you are always tripping over? Chances are the answer is yes. Yes, you might be able to dedicate some measly five minutes to throw something out. Sometimes that is all the time you need.

Imagine if you could read 2 – 3 pages in a book in about five minutes. Over time you could read a 600 page novel by sneaking in five minutes here and there. While you do other things that don't require your immediate attention, for example. Take a book with you everywhere you go and you can knock out a few pages while waiting in line for coffee. Another few pages while waiting in the grocery line or while you wait to pick up the kids. When we say that we don't have time we are usually making a negative excuse. Instead we ought to make positive excuses like, "Oh I have a few minutes to spare before I have to drive to work. Maybe I should take a look at the messy papers on my desk."

Tips and Tricks

- Remember about the principle of divide and conquer. Nobody says you have to do it all alone. You have your roommates, spouse or children who can help delegate chores. There are cleaning services that you can pay for while you are busy at work
- If something is so disused to the point that you have to wipe dust off the surface, its time to say goodbye
- Attics and closets only prolong the inevitable about decluttering. You will run out of free space in these areas eventually. Also note that

negative space is important inside of closets and attics as well. Imagine if you filled those spaces to their limit. If you wanted to remove anything stored you would have to take everything out on a last in, first out basis. That would take forever

- Money can replace most objects. Objects that can not be bought with money usually have sentimental value. These are the ones worth keeping
- Procrastination is made worse by easy access to pleasure. Limiting the available distractions around you can help with self-discipline
- Duplicate items take up too much space when you notice that you need to use last in, first out to reach your desired item

Activity Section

1. Difficult decisions take so much away from us in the form of time and opportunities. Make flipping a coin your new best friend. Get any coin, smartphone app or dice and get ready to make the plunge into quick decision resolutions. Whenever a hard decision comes up, just flip the coin—then decide what to do

based on the result. Simple. Easy. The task gets finished, its out of sight and out of mind. Time to relax.

2. Procrastination is a difficult beast to slay. Doing so might require a separate discussion but there are a few things you can do. One is to maintain a to-do list and follow it religiously. Every morning or afternoon you should have a list handy. Before you do anything, knock off the items in your list. The rest is just mental discipline

3. Identify a time block in your busy schedule, either in the morning or afternoon, that gives you five to ten minutes of free time. Get a timer out and within those 5 to ten minutes, do as much cleaning as humanly possible. You might surprise yourself at the sheer amount of tasks you can complete in such a short time. If you fail to finish, leave everything there and return next time. The more of these cleaning blocks you can dedicate throughout your day the more you can get finished

4. Become intimately related with your disuse category. What are the items that you don't use anymore? Why are they still in your house? Write down what these items are and when the last time you used them where. Keep these items in mind, because when it

comes to trash day these should be your first picks to get rid of.

Chapter 6: Thinking In Systems for Keeping The Home Clean

Systems thinking involves looking at the big picture rather than at small details. Every small part within that system works together to bring about the whole. Each part is equally important, but the system should be strong enough that it can function with the loss of a few parts. Systems are said to be reliable and fault tolerant. If something goes bad, there will be a backup process to keep things afloat. Failure should be avoided at all costs within that system. The only thing that matters is the continual operation of the system.

When we go about organizing the home the usual way is to look at details first, and then at the big picture later. There are "bad" areas that need lots of improvement while others aren't so bad. Or everything is equally bad, and everything has to be dealt with accordingly. Focusing on the details too much may cause one to feel burdened by the work. When we do see the whole, we tend to see it as a menacing problem that will take ages to fix. Then it becomes difficult or downright impossible to break the thing down into individual parts.

So we tackle the small details that really irk us. If the bedroom is disorderly, everything can be stuffed under the bed, shoved into drawers, and hidden from sight. If we are having guests over and the living room is a mess, the first instinct is to clear it out by putting things away in other rooms and then to throw away any trash. Each individual room has its own set of needs that ultimately determine how we treat the decluttering process. But looking at rooms as individual pieces robs you of the wholeness of the problem. You might feel that one room is okay being a little messy while keeping others clean.

There is a constant input and output process of objects within the home. Things enter through the front door and are distributed at random throughout the rooms. Some of these things end up leaving the home through the trash or recycling. They can also be given away. The bulk of what makes up clutter stays behind.

The entire home then, is a system of inputs and outputs. Just like somebody trying to lose weight is given the advice to eat less and move more, the idea is to keep the system in perfect balance between the inputs and the outputs. We can eat a bunch of ice cream if we wanted to. We could eat it everyday and the system that is our bodies would start to gain tons of weight. Then to get rid of that excess energy we need to start doing some movement. A lot of it, actually. Our bodies sweat but houses don't, and the only way to "burn off" the excess is to carefully select and cull what isn't needed.

Going room by room to fetch things for the trash is one way to do this, but in the end will be ineffective. Remember that things are constantly entering the home. Many times completely under our noses because we don't pay enough attention to what we bring inside. We don't pay attention to what others bring either. This is the same thing as eating out everyday and expecting exercise alone to show results. But we know that diet makes up 90% of weight loss. Some would say even more than that. It is much easier to eat less, while sticking to a workout routine and see better results. Doing so is the ideal solution in terms of effectiveness and efficiency.

It's a little more complicated when it comes to the home economy, though. For one, we eat for different reasons than why we buy things. We can also acquire new things through gifts and by literally picking up free stuff from the street. We can make things or transform old things into new creations entirely. Old things that break might get split into different pieces.

Whatever the case, these things end up filling up our homes. Caloric energy is needed to keep our bodies going, but past a certain point there is no need anymore. We buy things because we need them, or because we feel that we need them. Our needs are not concrete like the need to regrow cells and reproduce. We don't "need" to own luxuries for example. But since we like luxury items they have to be accounted for.

Some people could eat indefinitely if it wasn't for our stomachs that told us when to stop. Normally there isn't any mechanism to make us stop buying things besides our bank accounts. Our homes can't suddenly burp and tell us to stop bringing things inside. A spouse may complain here and there, but besides that there isn't anyone stopping us. Inside our bodies cells eventually got broken down and recycled. To us objects that break and no longer function are trash—so we throw them out. Objects that still work may cause a problem when we stop using them. They no longer seem to have a use and become functionally trash.

The health of a system depends on the processes that interact with each other. Each different part makes sure that the whole is working by performing a certain task. For every room in the house there is a certain process that takes place. At dinner time the kitchen becomes alight with activity. Food is transformed, trash gets taken out and the rest goes into our bodies. But even here we are making decisions that affect the entirety of the system.

When we eat on the couch for example, we are contributing to the mess of the house. Every time we bring a plate of food into a room we cause a pileup of dishes that need to be moved to their respective place. It's hard to keep track of all the objects in the house if they are out of place. Plates that go missing need to be rounded up.

Misplaced items are caused primarily through laziness. Laziness in turn is caused by a failure to create deliberate action. Deliberate action is the result of applied mindfulness. Harmony is created between individual parts of the home as you interact with them.

Functional Minimalism

Minimalism is the philosophy and global movement concerned with doing more with less. Less possessions, less furniture, less problems. The central idea of minimalism has to do with the art of constraint that you will learn more about in the next chapter. Constraints force us to think differently about individual property. It is asking what can we do with less. Or better yet, it's asking what functional aspect do we gain if we had less.

As a lifestyle choice minimalism is all about subtracting from the possessions pool. This could mean for example, having a smaller wardrobe. Instead of a cupboard filled with dishware, someone may own only a bowl, a plate and a single utensil. Because they put a premium on negative space they also won't need some of the creature comforts we take for granted today.

There has been a recent trend in only owning a single outfit. For example, someone may decide to wear only a faded pair of blue jeans and a black or white t-shirt. They then wear this outfit like a uniform to whatever occasion they deem fit. They still own many versions (or slightly different versions) of the same outfit but its still the same outfit in essence.

Most people would agree that this way of life is too extreme. Minimalism may work for some people, but it just doesn't appeal to the majority. Owning things is nice. There is nothing wrong with having a little material wealth lying around the house. Though minimalism can simplify our lives it can also make our lives well, boring. And not everyone wants that.

On the other hand we can think of a different type of minimalism, call it functional minimalism, that gives us some of the benefits of the lifestyle without making strong commitments. The goal of functional minimalism isn't to have less things, but to make better decisions. That way the clutter doesn't build up and we can keep it down for a long time. You don't necessarily have to throw anything out, but you will have to be careful about what you bring in.

Tenets of Functional Minimalism

1. ***Only bring as much as you bring out:*** Every time you introduce something into the home, something else should be removed. Preferably from the same category. EX: You buy vase for decoration. Get rid of something else you use for decoration.
2. ***Return after use:*** Every object that has been moved from its respective place should be returned to that location after use.
3. ***Last in never first out*:** This has to do with negative space and how the objects you own occupy it. Think about your closet or food pantry. Are you able to reach any given object without moving things around? Chances are that you can't. First you need to move the last thing you put in to make room.

Functional minimalism is being able to reach for and grab an item without causing a fuss. This also applies to the things you have laying around on your table, your shelves and in drawers. Items that are in display should have some buffer of negative space. You should be able to select items in storage using just one hand.

4. ***Simplicity over complexity:*** The home shouldn't be so complicated that we need a map to figure out where things are. Neither should we force ourselves to think hard about everyday decisions. There should always be one obvious way of doing things.

5. ***Fewer options over many:*** Options are the enemy of an anxious mind. The more options you have, the more difficult it is to make a decision. Limit the amount of functions that are dependent on singular items. You probably don't need a deep fryer appliance if you can perform the same function on the stove top. You probably don't need half a dozen of anything. Spices for example can clutter a kitchen counter. Pick your favorite three and ignore the rest.

6. ***Demonstrate an appreciation for negative space*:** When you decorate your home, there should be obvious signs of negative space.

Make a shrine that worships this space. Leave a wall bare if it doesn't provide any use. Don't put in random pieces of furniture. Don't buy anything that takes up too much space. People should be able to walk freely and breathe without knocking into things. There should be more than one path to get somewhere.

Making a System Out of It

A system has at its core, repetition and clearly defined inputs and outputs. You need to set aside time on a predefined schedule to help maintain a sense of functional minimalism throughout the house. This can be a weekly thing, daily or bi-weekly. Whatever works for you. What counts is that you make a conscious effort to follow the tenets discussed above. Maybe not at all once, but be looking around your house at areas that you can improve.

Follow your schedule to the letter. Carve out some twenty or thirty minutes each day. Dedicate this time towards converting your home into a state of functional minimalism. Do what needs to be done to follow the tenets, to the best of your ability. Expect slow progress at first and then rapid change. Expect a challenge and be prepared to make important decisions. Remember that the interval in between these sessions doesn't have to matter. Higher frequency is ideal in the beginning, then you can begin to ease things out towards one session a week, or if you are really good, one session a month.

As you continue with these regular sessions, you will begin to spot issues in between them. When things fall out of functional minimalism feel free to right them. Say you are making breakfast and you notice that your herbs and spices are so cluttered that you knock some over while preparing the food. This is a great opportunity to make a decision to get rid of some of these. They will fall into the trash with a satisfying clunk.

Don't stress things. Everything has to be simple, and there is nothing more simple than throwing something away in the trash. Replace things when needed but resist the urge to mend. A tablecloth that is old and lined with holes will not be easy to fix. Just throw it out and replace it with a new one. Choose the path of least resistance.

Tips and Tricks

- Make it a habit to clean, organize and right things as you do everyday activities. Avoid the tendency to clean up "all at once"

- The longer you stick to a system, the easier it becomes to follow
- Things get better with the passing of time. Functional minimalism will be difficult at first because your organizational burden is high. In a few weeks or months things will start running smoothly
- The health of the system favors that things be simple. If you get stuck with a difficult task or decision, move on to something else. It's more important to keep things going than to have all the answers
- Continual maintenance of functional minimalism is as much a lifestyle as it is a chore. Your actions should reflect it. Just like you take care of plants, your home needs to be taken care of too

Activity Section

1. There is no right or wrong way to perform one of these sessions described above. Remember what the tenets are, and do your best to follow them. As practice, stop whatever you are doing and dedicate some 20 minutes to perform one of these sessions. Fill

your mind with the idea of simplicity as you go. Try to feel the harmony as you right things around the house. You can either focus on the house entirely or a certain area. This is your way of fighting back against clutter.

2. As you try out the sessions, avoid bringing anything new into the house. Remember that functional minimalism says to always keep the inputs and outputs of the home in perfect balance. That way no additional things get added and the organizational burden stays the same throughout.

3. Go through your wardrobe and get rid of anything that is old or that doesn't fit. If the clothes are still perfectly wearable, put these in a large plastic bag and forget about them. Then when you have the time drop them off at your local clothes charity. Throw out any old undergarments that are old.

4. Throw out any shoes that you don't need. Remember the law of categories and how they might apply to your footwear. You don't really need more than one pair of running shoes or sneakers. Always be limiting the amount of possible options.

5. Take a critical look at your dishware. At most, you only need one mug per person in the home. Perhaps a few dishes per person, and

maybe three pieces of utensils per each. There should be harmony inside of the house as well as in those areas that aren't visible like the cupboard.

6. Find one miscellaneous category of things you own and try to simplify it. Limit the available options. If you have four different types of shampoos, trim it down to only two. Do the same for types of cereals you have, jewelry, etc.

Chapter 7: Mental Models for Helping You Stay Organized

Everyday life can be confusing to our mind's eye. We like to think we know what the nature of reality is but find that some things have no explanation. We don't always look for answers unless they are easy to figure out. Our mind has the tendency to make up explanations to help us make sense of the world. For every how there is some metaphysical why we tend towards. This can occur in the back of our subconscious while we pay attention to something else.

The brain is our primary link to reality when you think about it. Everything has color or sound because our brain tells us that they do. We create little models of reality in our head because we are pattern recognizing creatures. Models help us make decisions about reality. Probably the most famous model is the 80 /20 rule. The rule states that for any given thing, there is a tendency for 80 percent of it being caused by 20 percent. For example in wealth distribution, 80% percent of the land can be owned by a small 20% of people. In competitive wild species, 20% of the fittest males are said to match with 80% of the fittest females for optimal reproduction.

The 80/20 rule is also known as the Pareto principle, and it is a type of mental model. Mental models are everywhere and people who have knowledge of them are able to make better decisions than people who do not. Another possible mental model is using the power of small, tiny habits. Over time these habits add to much more. If you are paying attention you will notice that tiny habits can be construed as another way of stating the Pareto principle. Maybe the distribution isn't exactly 80/20 in this case, but you see how the logic still stands. A small minority can have a large impact.

Mental models are a favorite among entrepreneurs and business people because they are interested in getting things done. In the long run mental models make everything more efficient and you are able to accomplish more. They might help you ace a test or learn a new language quickly. In the wild there are several hundreds of these models and much has already been written about them. Entire books are dedicated to individual models if they are important enough.

In the spirit of decluttering we can apply some of these models to help things go by smoothly. Most mental models are not the perfect solution to your problems but they can still be effective. They give you some idea of what is going on, why things happen and how you can gain an edge by applying those principles.

A mental model need not be overly complex. They are just another way of saying "idea", but in a broader context that can be related to something specific. In this case, decluttering. Mental models shouldn't be a scary thing to adopt. Just pay attention to what the model is saying and figure out how you can use it.

Birds of a Feather

The number one rule of organization says that like things go together. There is a certain harmony between things that are alike and a certain disharmony among things that are different. We see this everywhere in life not just in interior design. There is an idea of entropy, or disorder that states that any system tends to get more and more disorderly over time. This is the second law of thermodynamics. If you start with something that is evenly distributed the molecules will spread out in random direction. For example, imagine a toddler using finger paint. The blank canvas is like the negative space in your home. Pristine, untouched and unbothered. Then we introduce a little disorder by having the toddler add some color. Then another color. And then another. Soon the canvas is no longer white, but mixture of every color available. This is disorder in action.

For our homes we want neither perfect order nor complete disorder. The harmony lies somewhere in the middle. Instead of making a total mess with the paints, we ask the toddler to draw us a picture of an elephant. It isn't necessary to completely fill the canvas with color. We can see that there is some sense of order to the canvas now.

So how do we keep the measure of disorder uniform, so that we can still tell what the picture is telling us? One possible way is to put similar ideas together. All that a picture is doing is communicating some emotion or idea to the viewer. In the case of the elephant the idea concerns a four legged land animal with tusks and a long trunk for a nose.

In our homes we could try doing the same, by communicating the form and the function of the things we surround ourselves with. This goes back to the idea of categories. But it isn't enough to simply put things in place according to how they relate. They must also communicate an overall idea. Birds of a feather flock together. All the things in your house perform a dance.

An object needs purpose both in its relation to other objects and with negative space. A stool should be used for sitting not for piling things on top of it. Or for storing things underneath it. It should go with the other stools. Maybe as part of a table set. At the very least it should be placed somewhere that makes sense to sit on.

Throughout the rest of your house you may find objects like this that have no relation to thought or purpose. They got into the position that they find themselves in because of careless decisions on your part. There is no harmony there, only disorder that steadily increases. Forget any reasons why you might have put the object there, or what the object means to you. If it doesn't follow form or function then there is something wrong.

This mental model outlines a central dilemma in decluttering. On the one hand you have the quantity dimension, where having too much things causes problems. On the other hand you have the purpose dimension, where having things out of place causes its own set of problems. If something is out of place it also contributes to the loss of negative space by default.

Remember that birds of a feather flock together. When its time to migrate, large flocks of birds travel as one in perfect formation. Likewise, objects in your home should exhibit a similar harmony both in their form and their purpose.

A Box of Spare Parts

When talking about a category of disuse we mean all those objects that cease to have utility. They are forgotten for whatever reason. But they are not disposed of because they have some redeeming quality. It is this strange quality they have that they might be deemed useful for certain purposes. A spare is synonymous with a duplicate, like the spare tire that we keep in the trunk of the car. It has a purpose, but only in certain scenarios.

A box of spare parts then, is the idea of keeping things we might need for later. But notice here that the box is singular and not plural. If you have multiple boxes of disused items your are somewhere in between moving in and moving out. But a singular box allows you to pack as many things as you can while at the same time conserving space. This box can then go in the attic or in the garage and you can forget about it. Everything else that doesn't fit should get thrown in the trash.

This is also where you should put any duplicates that make no sense being somewhere else. It makes sense to keep a black pen on your desk, it doesn't make sense to keep an entire container of pens there. These are often so cheap that they are sold in packs. Once out the pack they get everywhere and serve no additional purpose. So stuff these in your box of spare parts and then forget about them.

Other miscellaneous items can go in here as well but be careful—these objects will have limited access. It doesn't make sense to put rolls of toilet paper there because those are often needed. Just those small trinkets throughout the house that seem to litter desks and counters. They bring disorder to negative space when you don't want it.

A box of spare parts doesn't have to be a literal box, of course. It could be any container or even section in your closet. Ideally it is out of sight from the rest of the home and compact enough that it doesn't impede the function of its surrounding objects. It will be there waiting for you on a rainy day.

The Law of Diminishing Returns

Have you ever experienced something so good that you just had to try it again and again? And then upon trying it for a second or third time the feeling wasn't so great? This is the law of diminishing returns. It states that a return on investment is greatest once a product can fulfill a need, but that purchasing that product X additional times will have a lesser effect. In other words, the first glass of water you drink after a long run feels much better than any other water you drink after that.

Duplicates in your house won't make you any happier beyond a certain point. Nor will duplicates of ideas, or items that seek to fulfill needs that have already been met. Collectors items can be a hard sell if you can't control their spread. Liquor cabinets fill niche role of storing your bottles. Everything is neat and contained. But what you happens when you come to own more bottles that actually fit? The liquor cabinet is now useless because you have new items entering the negative space of your home. The extra bottles aren't doing anything for you—they just contribute to more clutter.

A similar scenario occurs with collections of DVD's, records, and old tapes. These physical items have little use by themselves. They require some piece of technology to work. And beyond a certain point additional items don't increase satisfaction. Though these things are nice to have, they aren't worth cluttering your space if you won't use them often. Consider also the fact that some of them can be digitized and their physical copies thrown out.

When you are in the process of decluttering a room keep in mind the law of diminishing returns. What do you have that is essentially a clone of something else, either in form or in purpose? Electronics are a big offender of diminishing returns. Every year there seems to be a new product on the market that is better than what it was the previous year. Whenever we upgrade these items we sometimes hang on to the old ones for some reason. Having two phones makes virtually no difference in most cases.

The law of diminishing returns may also be applied to organizational implements like drawers, files, and see through storage bins. Most of these implements will take up a sizable portion of negative space and they all perform the same function. Sure you can store more things if you have more of them, but at what costs? Why are you storing things in the first place? The purpose of these implements is to hide from plain view objects that shouldn't be visible out in the open. They also help you organize things (birds of a feather) in neat sections.

But at a certain point having additional storage crosses the line between harmony and disharmony. Your house shouldn't look like a museum archive. It's unclear whether they contribute more to order or disorder.

Instead of focusing on needs that have already been met, consider branching out to other avenues. What's something you always wanted to try? Are there any improvements you can make to the home itself? The purpose of life should be to always keep things fresh by varying the experience. Buying the same things over and over goes against this. If you introduce variation in a healthy way, then the law of diminishing returns will never need to affect you negatively.

The Art of Constraints

Every once in a while a writer or artist will reach a block in their creative process where they can't think about any new ideas. A block can last for temporary periods but it can also extend for years and years. It's not that the artist has run out of talent but that their minds simply cannot find inspiration the same way it did before. It is terrible thing that can end creative careers.

One technique for getting over an artistic block is to think in terms of constraints. An artist may decide to use only one color in their work, or to only use lines. A writer may constrain themselves to only write about one character or use the same setting throughout their work. You would be surprised what the human mind can come up with when under the duress of having fewer options. You might find new techniques or uses for objects that you never knew where there.

Constraints are well know to people who come from poor backgrounds. When forced to do more with less, the brain unlocks a new set of creative faculties that are hidden for people who have plenty. If there is no need to come up with creative solutions it usually means that something else is there to satisfy it. Imagine somebody wants to get into fitness but they can't afford a gym. They also can't afford any equipment for their home. But they have an old broomstick and empty milk jugs lying around. Filling the jugs with something heavy like sand or concrete and then sticking them on the end of the broom results in makeshift weights.

Having less creates less options. Having less options makes you think on your feet. Both of these ideas resonate with functional minimalism and mindfulness which we have been talking about the entire book. The mental model of constraints can be applied to almost anywhere in the home. Simply removing an object or a need that you have in the home creates a constraint. If you have too much of one thing, you can put up an artificial constraint.

For example, one constraint could be to limit the amount of boxes you have lying around. You will be forced to think about creative ways to use the stuff inside the boxes. You could also choose to wear less styles of clothing so that when you shop you only buy certain apparel. Pretty much anything can be a constraint. If you think about it, the whole of minimalism is built on the idea that you can do more with less. Or that having less is having more.

Certainly you can expect to have more opportunities if you have less options. You become better able to use what you already have. Nothing gets neglected or forgotten. There is always a use, always a why to the things you own.

Using constraints will help your creative juices flow. Literally any change you make in the home will be attenuated by the art of constraint because now you have to think with purpose. The beauty of artificial constraints is that you can go back on them whenever you wish. If something doesn't work out there is always the option of reversing the constraint.

Tips and Tricks

- Experiment with these mental models as you see fit. They are by no means perfect. Feel free to modify them, or come up with new ones
- Mental models should be used as guidelines and never the end all, be all solution
- Form follows function is an old idea in architecture. Basically, it means that the shape of a building should fit the function it seeks to fulfill. The idea has since spread to other disciplines as well

- Spare parts are intended as a lifeline not as an excuse to stockpile useless items
- One way to keep diminishing returns low is to constantly rotate the items that you use the most in the house. If you primarily use a certain piece of furniture consider swapping it out. Redecorate the house often
- Artificial constraints will require some degree of willpower if the constraint is a pain point. It's for the same reason that so many fail diets. Constraints are powerful, but they require some degree of discipline. So be prepared for making these changes

Activity Section

1. Take a look at the objects in your house and examine where form is following function. How do objects interact with the built environment and with people? See if you can identify places where form isn't following function. What category is being representing by that object, and how can you return this object to be with its flock?

   Find objects that appear to be in the "wrong" and carefully right them. Common areas you may wish to look at are pieces of furniture that have become storage centers, bicycle handles that are being used to hang clothes and other miscellaneous items that aren't following their purpose. A napkin holder overstuffed with old mail, a lonesome bookend that has been misplaced. A tangle of electronic equipment and wires that have become hopelessly entwined.

2. Go around various rooms looking for what you deem as spare parts. These can belong to a disuse category or they may simply be objects that you haven't gotten the opportunity to use in a while. Old hobby and arts and crafts pieces may go here. Glue, rarely used scotch tape and extra stationery are good options. Spare parts are by nature miscellaneous. Avoid putting things that belong to larger collections, like tools or cleaning supplies.
3. Things that go together should stay together. And yet they seem to sprout legs and walk into other rooms by their own. Take some time to send those sheep back with their flock.
4. Play a quick game of object poker. In the game of poker cards are related to each other in terms of rank and suit. All suits have the

same characteristics (spades, diamonds, clubs and hearts) and similar ranks form a quartet (four sevens). Objects likewise belong to general categories and can have a rank (the amount of objects).

In object poker the goal is to find the highest amount of like pairs as possible. Things in the same category with the most duplicates are absolute winners. As a reward give them the gift of release. The longest chains of pairs that you make give you a hint about what should be removed.

Of course there are some exceptions. Object poker is a good exercise to examine with a plain view what your inventory is. Someone who adores books will have lots of them, but they can learn how to store them without contributed to the mess. Problems tend to arise only when there are many objects that have high ranks. One or two are still manageable.

5. Somethings finding the right constraints is an exercise in itself. They should be creative, but they should also have some bearing on what your problems are. If you suffer from specific pain points now is the time to address them. Awareness of others is a good place to start.

If someone has ever told you that you have too much of this thing, or that your collections are too big it may be time to listen.

Other constraints may simply come out of the blue. If you can't think about any, pick at least one from the following and implement the changes.

A. Constraint of Dishware – Limit dishware according to how many people live in the household. Two dishes per person, two cups, one mug, or some other variation that you see fit.

B. Constraint of Space – Stick to the rule of three or two. At most, you will have objects directly touching each other or in close proximity only in groups of two or three. Say goodbye to your cluttered bathroom sinks full of cramped beauty supplies. Instead space them out adequately.

C. Constraint of Old – Redecorate a room in your house by moving furniture around but do not buy anything new. You are free to get rid of old things if it makes the room look better, but that is all.

D. Constraint of Time – Identify which objects or groups of objects that take up most of your time. When you interact with them next them put a hard cap on the amount of time you use them for. Say one or two hours. Using specific things for less time allows you to use other things you wouldn't normally notice.

Chapter 8: How To Actually Clean Your House

The next biggest goal after decluttering your home is being able to "finally" clean your home. The nature of clutter is that it makes us feel dirty even after the house has been cleaned. Clutter will impede the cleaning process because there is less surface area that you can physically reach. Areas of the walls, floors and hard to reach places may never get touched. Cleaning the home goes hand in hand with decluttering that these subjects can't be logically separated.

It goes against the title of the chapter but there isn't one "right" way to clean. There is however, a distinctive wrong way. Cleaning the house but not doing anything about clutter is hardly cleaning at all.

Lazy cleaning would be a better term for it. Because the clutter hasn't left the house it's as if you forgot to clean up all the trash.

It is often effective to clean up and clear any clutter as you go. You will have to wear two hats while you do this. One hat is your regular cleaning hat you wear when you give the house a good scrub down. This is fairly standard to anyone who has ever tried to "deep clean" their homes. You have your mop, your vacuum, your scrubs, detergents and window wiper. The second hat is your decluttering hat, the skills of which you have developed by reading through this book and performing the exercises.

Recall that each room in your house has a distinct purpose. That means you should adopt different cleaning strategies demeaning on what room you clean. A kitchen should not be treated like a bedroom and so on. Because they are different, some rooms will have an optimal way of cleaning than others. You will need to use special equipment for some. In the end the best you can do is stick to a plan.

Cleaning in The Age of Clutter

Cleaning the home is like an oxymoron if clutter is still a problem. There is a sense that something is wrong even though you just finished scrubbing every corner. Part of it is because objects take up space and most of us are not willing to lift everything up and clean under them. Some percentage of the surface area found in a room will always be occupied by your things. Objects with high inertia like large pieces of furniture are hard to clean around. Smaller objects can have inertia too because you haven't used them in a while. You don't notice them, much less clean under them.

Tidying up alongside the clutter and without removing the clutter can be tricky. The ideal situation is to first lift everything up and then clean. But because there are so many things, you can bet the house will look completely different upon putting things back where they were.

Under our systems way of thinking it becomes impractical to clean up all at once. Small tweaks here and there are the way to go. The consequence of this is that the house takes longer to truly clean. But once its clean and free from clutter, maintaining that level of cleanliness is a walk in the park.

The Arsenal

For many of us the idea of manually dusting the house is near impossible. There are simply too many rooms, too many things in those rooms, and too many hard to reach places. You should be able to recognize that these issues are all the opposite of functional minimalism. A home that conforms to the tenants of functional minimalism is actually very easy to clean. You will have wide open spaces and plenty of buffer in between objects that dusting the house actually makes sense. In the meantime you should do what you can with what you got.

All you really need to "clean" a house are a bristle broom, mop and a handheld duster or brush. This will cover most of the floor, walls and windows. Dusting implements can be as simple as handheld towel wipes that you get rid of afterwards. More specialty products are available as well, but you can get away with just the wipes.

This will take care of the small debris that collects over time (and gets all over neglected items). For the kitchen you should also have plastic gloves, dish detergent, some cleaning agents (like vinegar, lime, off the shelf product) and baking soda. The same with the bathroom. Bleach and Clorox based cleaners work well for the bathtub and toilet. Next you might want to keep on hand some natural deodorizers like herbs and powder. Baking soda works well. Essentially this is all you need. Your cleaning supplies should be maintained regularly or downright replaced if maintenance is too much of a bother. Brooms and mops are cheap enough to replace every year.

Dust will always be an issue. The only good way to get rid of it is by regularly going over the house, top to bottom, and getting rid of it manually. Do this more often and dust will stay down. Linens and bed sheets need to be washed regularly and dusted. Some rooms are more prone to dust because of their construction or proximity to the outdoors. In those cases you might consider an air purifying device. Lastly, if you have central heating and cooling make sure you regularly switch our filters, preferably with HEPA complaint ones.

The Living Room

Logistically this is the largest room in your home in most cases. Cleaning it can be a breeze or a nightmare. Resist the urge to put things in the living room simply because there is more space there. Out of all of the rooms, this area should be the barest. It is where guests come to visit and a space for clearing your mind. Keep the furniture to a minimum and allow negative space to flourish.

Begin by giving a thorough brooming. Don't bother trying to moved "fixed" objects that normally stay on the ground. Work around and under furniture. If you wish to declutter things only remove those objects you that you don't intend on putting back. Instead trash them.

Wipe surfaces twice starting from the ceiling and then going down until the room is finished. Clean furniture off separately but only if those surfaces are dirty or odorous.

But before you do anything, remove any items that don't belong in the living room. Toys, extra blankets taken from bedrooms, pillows and food related items don't belong here. Keep nick knacks to a minimal and explore different harmony with mementos you might display. If you must decorate walls remember to control for negative space. Don't aim to overwhelm with your decorations as these make cleaning walls bothersome.

Kitchen and Sink

A hallmark of a well run house is having a spotless kitchen. Which is rare these days because more people work and don't have time to scrub every last spot. Kitchens get dirty easy primarily through food preparation. Be especially mindful not to leave food scraps out in the open where they can rot. Scraps should be refrigerated, thrown out, or put towards compost.

Aim to keep your surfaces clean and to minimize the amount of clutter on counter tops. There should be plenty of negative space in the kitchen to comfortably get around and prepare food. The biggest offenders in this space are kitchen appliances like blenders, food processors, toasters and coffee makers. The best case scenario is to integrate appliances with the build environment if possible, like a microwave that has been built-in to a shelf.

Appliances should be organized according to their use. The coffee maker is probably used most frequently, so it makes sense for it to be on the counter. Other less commonly used items should be stowed away in their compartments. If you own too many of these appliances then over time there won't be any space for them. This is a mistake you should avoid.

The best way to declutter these items is to have a critical look at what their use cases are, and seeing if there is overlap with other appliances or traditional cookware. Some top of the line pressure cookers can perform many of the functions that a slow cooker can, for example. If space is limited, make decisions between which appliances should stay.

Fridge And Pantry

Having too much food in the home is wasteful and a bad allocation of resources. You only need enough food for one or two weeks. Things will still go bad in the fridge, especially if left for days and weeks. Dry goods tend to keep for longer. These are products like grains, legumes, cereals and canned goods. Snack food is also included in this category. Such foods can be kept for many months or even years in some cases. Remember the tenet from functional minimalism about the last in first out principle. Within the tight confines of your fridge and pantry you should have ample space to select items without knocking things over.

In practical terms tight spaces are difficult to optimize for negative space. So you shouldn't feel too bad if you have to move the eggs and the milk to get the juice from the fridge. However, if you design these spaces to accommodate enough buffer, you will struggle less with food preparation.

Bathroom

Probably everyone's least favorite room to clean, the bathroom is also prone to clutter. In particular the sink area. Since many bathrooms have small confined spaces, clutter becomes a bigger issue than in other rooms. It's no fun at all trying to clean the bathroom when the surfaces have been stacked with cosmetic and hygiene items. These items need to be picked up, and then reorganized with each clean of the bathroom.

A better solution is to keep the clutter as low as possible. Substitute products for each other if possible and make decisions about which to keep. Much of our soaps, shampoos and skin cleaning products are purchased on whim. Meanwhile other items that we forgot about still have plenty of product left inside them. Finish old containers before buying new ones.

The ideal bathroom is a cool, mellow place that shouldn't cause any anxieties. Nobody likes to feel anxious when they are sitting on the toilet. Allowing for ample negative space reduces anxiety, so does reducing the number of options that are presented. Again the solution here isn't to stuff everything underneath the medicine cabinet but instead to be selective. Only keep the most important items in the bathroom at a single time. Toothbrushes, toothpaste, hand soap, floss and other bare essentials should be sparse. If sharing the bathroom consider having a rule where everyone needs to take care of their own personal items. There are plenty of small travel bags that can fit creams, toothbrushes, shaving supplies and other items. They are compact and inexpensive.

Tips and Tricks

- Bedrooms should follow the same protocols as the living room but on a smaller scale. Since there is more personal taste involved this will be up to the reader
- Certain types of flooring/drapery will invite more dust to your home. Hardwood floors are generally your best bet, while shag carpets are the worst. If you must have carpet avoid covering the entire house in it. Opt in for quality materials
- Clutter and dust go hand in hand as symptoms of a home that is being neglected

Activity Section

1. If you haven't already, give your fridge a complete and total deep cleanse. Seldom do we think about the forgotten leftovers way back in the recesses of the fridge. Take inventory of what is currently in the fridge and for how long it has been there. Items that are difficult to date are your problem foods.

Make a note of buying less of those. Consider investing in a large ice cooler or borrow one from a friend. You don't want your food to spoil as you do your thing.

2. Pick one room in your house and perform a similar deep cleanse. Get rid of any clutter along the way if it is particularly bad. You can quickly sweep a room down for a good clean by using a three box method. Get any three different containers. One will be for items that are out of place, another for items that you will toss, and a third for items that you intend to get rid of but that you feel bad throwing away.

   Within the first few moments of staring focus on getting things inside of those three boxes first. Once everything has been picked up, go in with your arsenal of cleaning supplies and give the room a run for its money. After the manual cleaning is finished, start putting things back from the out of place box. Throw away everything in the toss box. And keep the items in the last box for later. You will have to pick a time to donate these or sell them. This last box can be reused as you go through your other rooms as well.

   After you complete a deep clean of one room,

see what your mood is like. Some people find that getting one thing done builds momentum, and they get excited for moving on to the next task. But if you feel tired and spent, save the other rooms for another occasion.

Chapter 9: Maintaining Harmony

It does not matter how slowly you go as long as you do not stop. - Confucius

At a certain point along your journey you will notice clutter begin to disappear. It could be tomorrow, a week from now or six months in the future. Suddenly you can see more of your house than ever before. Bare walls make themselves known and the floor extends to previously unknown dimensions. Your furniture and counter tops are free from stray objects. There is no lingering feeling that you are indebted to your objects. For once in a long time, you feel yourself becoming attuned to a new type of harmony throughout your home.

But reader beware. For this feeling is not everlasting should you ever reach that point of nirvana. Harmony requires constant maintenance of the junk in and around the home. Corners need to be swept, shelves organized and objects returned to their proper resting points. Serious decisions need to be made about the overall presentation of the home and especially about its contents. So far in this book we have covered various ways to achieve this but you may still be wondering how to put it all together. In essence, the maintenance of the home can be summed up by taking all pieces from the previous chapters and putting them together.

As soon as you stop maintaining the home the same old disorder from before takes a hold. More objects enter the home. They then become disorganized by the passing of the days in which you forget that they exist. Life happens, and your radar shifts to more important matters like family, work and personal health. Little by little clutter starts to pile up again with the subversion of your attention. You can prevent all this by sticking to the habits that you have been working on throughout this book.

Your priorities may change, and you may no longer wish to maintain the home like before now that it is clean. If you feel like this is an issue you need to tweak the formula to suit your needs. Once you reach that point of total declutter there is no reason why clutter should return. Nor should it seem like an enormous task to declutter when necessary. You already did the hard part. Assuming you followed the tenants of functional minimalism and reduced the rate of acquiring new things there should be little left in your way.

You need to catch yourself whenever you feel your attention wandering. It's okay to wander, but always exercise the power to bring your attention back. Remember what you set out to in the beginning. What did you intend for your home to look like? What sort of order did you hope for? Organizational goals are for life just as minimalism is a lifestyle in itself.

An Accumulation of Habits Not of Things

Maintenance sounds like a lousy activity because our views of maintenance have to do with work. The first thing that comes to mind are the armies of custodians that clean our office spaces every night. In the morning everything is clean yet we take it for granted. We are old enough to know this doesn't happen by magic. There aren't little gnomes who come out when nobody is looking to pick up after the rest of society. Most of this work is done by unskilled laborers trying to earn a living. Because of their efforts we can enjoy orderly public spaces.

Unless you live in a relatively large place, you won't need extra help. This is especially true if you continue to think about decluttering like a system of habits. Cleaning a little bit here, organizing a little there. Household chores are generally straight forward and are rarely the hard part. These can be delegated to other members of the household when necessary. What poses the greatest challenge is dealing with your clutter. Both in terms of managing existing clutter and in terms of preventing future clutter from occurring. Heck, admitting that clutter is a problem is difficult enough.

To this end we can think of a general set of guidelines that aim to satisfy these requirements. First, we must find the level of harmony that we are comfortable with. Think back to the first chapter where we discussed a formula for success. You learned about the four truths of decluttering, including truth number four: everyone is different. Figure out just how much clutter you want to get rid of and then go from there.

Think about it as different levels along a functional minimalism spectrum. A home that follows some of the tenets will look a certain way, and a home that follows all of the tenets will look different still. On one end you have a vision of a completely minimalist household and on the other you have a vision of total disorder.

Once you have that target, its time to divide and conquer. Identify trouble areas and break them down into their bare essentials. Where did the clutter come from? How long has this clutter been affecting you? And what systems must you put in place so that this clutter never returns?

Everything In Balance

Ultimately the only thing that can save you from clutter is balance. Balance and harmony are two synonyms of the same ideal. One is to be at peace with your mind (harmony) and the other is to be at peace with your actions (balance). Only after mastering balance will you be able to feel harmony. Balance follows from your principles, which in turn determine your daily decisions.

You shouldn't buy too much of one thing. You shouldn't ignore the state of the home. And you shouldn't over or under estimate your needs. Balance is difficult to achieve for so many because we have changing schedules. We favor some priorities over others like work over relationships. Or money over experiences. Too much of our time is spent on less meaningful tasks like scrolling through our phones.

Addictive behavior can develop in a heartbeat, whether it is a shopping addiction or addiction to technology. Throw in procrastination into the mix and you have the makings of the worst habits imaginable for clutter to take over. A consolidating effort is required to overcome these tendencies.

Do not underestimate the power of making checklists. Try to remember your days in secondary school where everything was regimented by the sound of the bell. Back then you probably hated the idea that your day could be split into blocks of time. But it isn't that terrible of an idea. A daily schedule keeps your actions in line with your priorities. Following the schedule is the hard part.

A schedule can help you avoid procrastination. If you know ahead of time the things you need to get done, there is less cognitive load associated with starting. Often it is this initial blimp of uncertainty that prevents us from being productive. There are so many distractions around us that we get lost in them. The mind becomes drunk with the promise of entertainment and pleasure. But if you set goals for yourself coupled with an adequate reward system these distractions won't seem appealing. Doing nothing to address problems is a rotten feeling. Actively trying to fix problems is tedious, but the payoff is worth it.

The Declutter Troubleshooting Checklist

What if you followed everything discussed in this book and the clutter just keeps coming back? There could be a number of problems at work. Always revisit the formula from chapter one and the four truths. Many of these issues arise from there. You can also use this checklist for general troubleshooting.

1. ***Bad Shopping Habits***: You are buying too more things relative to your needs. You might buy on a whim, because you saw something you just had to have. Fixing this requires a careful consideration of what products mean to you.

2. ***Pack Rat Mentality:*** You are scared that throwing things away means losing something. This is more common with people who come from poor backgrounds. You have to eliminate this fear because you gain more from a decluttered home than having useless items.

3. ***Sentimental Attachment***: You have a strong emotional bond to a disproportionate amount of items. This and the issue above have to do with indecisiveness. It's fine to have mementos or things we are attached to. It is not fine, or normal to grow attached to

everyday things. Maybe you still have your first frying pan from when you moved out to college. Chose wisely which items are important and which ones you can throw away. As a last resort, consider taking photographs of these items and creating online backups. That way you can relive the memories without having the physical burden of ownership.

4. ***Mental Illness***: You are going through a rough patch and don't have the energy to declutter. The age old question is which one came first, depression and anxiety or clutter? In either case performing a deep clean of your belongings is very therapeutic. Throwing away old things linked to old memories is one of the most liberating things you can do to get better. Don't sweat it.

5. ***Failure to Make a System:*** You reach some level of clutter-free living and then old habits return. You are too busy, or your priorities are out of whack. Making a checklist is vital if you fall under this category. A checklist will either make a break a person. You may feel that checklists are gimmicks or waste of time. But it takes very little to make one. Every night before you go to bed or first thing in the morning make one. Knock off those tasks

that you have been putting off and don't do anything until they are finished.

6. ***Not Using Technology to Your Advantage:*** Technology definitely has its uses and will continue to do so in the coming years. Your smartphone can help you with timers, making checklists and tracking your progress. You can already find many apps that help you record your clutter. But if that doesn't interest you a low tech solution involves taking pictures over time. Images in your smartphone get automatically timestamped so you can organize them by date. In addition to those images you can write notes and even insert images into them.

7. ***Going at it Alone:*** We all need support systems to help us fulfill our goals. If this support system is missing you will have greater difficulty achieving your goals. At the very least, discuss your goals with friends and loved ones. See what they have to say.

8. ***Falling Into the Thrift Trap:*** We all like a good deal. A favorite pastime of the middle class has always been to go out thrifting. Establishments that sell second hand goods are extremely popular. From public donation based stores to stores that sell marked down items. Online you can find tons of cheap

"irregular" clothing that have small factory imperfections. The problem as you can probably guess, is that we spend more if things cost less.

Resist the notion that cheap goods are necessary. If they fit your needs, then go ahead and buy. But once those needs are met don't just buy more things.

9. ***Not Buying Quality Items***: Buying the wrong things can also pose a problem. Our needs can be met with a certain product and then suddenly it breaks. Now you have to figure out what to do with the old item and need to procure a new one. Clothes is a notorious offender. Look for quality items that are built to last. Avoid the mentality that tech products must be upgraded each year.

10. ***An Elephant Living In a Mouse's House:*** We can't always afford the space that we would like. Rents are rising just about everywhere in the world. Apartments now cost what houses used to. The consequence is that there is less space available for tenants. One could even trace the rise in market prices alongside the rise in the popularity of minimalism.

    Not that there is a problem with apartments

themselves. The problem are people living in small areas with the mentality that they can fit more and more things. People who move from bigger houses to smaller ones vastly underestimate how much decluttering they have to make.

Remember the sanctity of negative space. You can have an organized home but without the necessary breathing room you will still feel surrounded by clutter. Only instead of small miscellaneous items you have larger than life furniture pieces that simply don't fit.

11. ***Still Being Stuck On Autopilot*:** Maybe you still have difficulty making mindful decisions everyday. This issue is synonymous with those long drives we take to visit someone far away. Since driving for long periods is tedious, many cars have a cruise-control feature where the car maintains its speed on its own. This is the same thing as autopilot. But when you are the only car driving along the highway there aren't many interesting decisions to make.

    Real life is completely different. And if you continue to make automatic decisions they might just bite you on your butt. Getting out of autopilot is a matter of escaping your own thought process, which is achievable through meditation and mindfulness.

12. ***You Procrastinate:*** So you've reached a reasonable balance of negative space and most of your clutter is gone. Then for whatever reason, you simply stop paying attention. The maintenance of the home stagnates as the days go on by. The initial levels of comfort you got from cleaning were so good that you simply decided to stop. After all, why should you continue your efforts if you reached your goal already?

    Ask any professional athlete what would happen to their bodies if they simply decided to give up. Their muscles shrink. Performance suffers. Athletes are driven individuals that understand how important it is to keep going even after initial goals have been met.

    Though unlike the athlete, maintaining a clutter free home doesn't require insane amounts of dedication. We simply choose not to because well, there are better things to do. And for many "clean enough" really is enough.

    Here there is a trade-off between having a home that looks good enough and one that is pristine year round. It's up to the reader to decide which one they prefer. Many readers will be satisfied with simply reducing the clutter they have.

Conclusion

Clutter has become a standard fact of life for so many of us. Too many accept it as an inevitable quality of owning or renting a home. The truth is that clutter becomes an extension of individual habits and no more. They are the decisions that we make when we are tired and beat up from doing daily life activities that cause us to forget about our things. We ask where did that pile of old clothes come from? Or why do I have so many pans if I only use one or two? We never ask the questions that really matter. Like what our needs are, what our long-term goals are, and what we should expect from our home life.

Hopefully you have found the answers to some of these questions by reading through the chapters provided. These are not by any means easy questions to answer. They are the kind that may take a lifetime to truly find the correct response. But don't fret. Nobody says that you must have the answers now. What matters is that you take an active role in determining how these factors affect the state of the home. You can still do so much even without knowing the answers.

Courage can go a long way. Change doesn't happen overnight but mustering that courage to move forward is the first step. Consider those who suffer from a clutter problem and never get it fixed. They can go all through all their lives paying a mortgage and still have a less than beautiful home on the inside. To them the option to declutter probably never manifested as a real option. And now consider yourself, dear reader, and how you have already made a step towards fixing that problem. Compared to them, you are already half way towards finding harmony in your home with your things and your family.

The sky is only the limit from this point on. What comes next when your home is finally sorted? You can try new hobbies and crafts to do around the house. You can add new additions and projects that make negative space pop out. Now that you have done something about the inside of the home, you can focus on the external parts. If you are so interested, you can deepen your knowledge about design and architecture. In so doing you will find some of the same concepts we talked about here, like the purpose of space and how form should follow function.

You can also help others to organize their own homes should the opportunity arise. The knowledge that you learn is meant to be shared, as this book has shared it with you. Now that you have embarked on the journey you can help others get there too. The clutter that others hold on to are like the spiny roots on a tree. Troublesome and needing to be pruned. If you see somebody suffering from clutter, offer to help them be able to breathe again.

Minimalism has began a new revolution in the way we decorate the home and lifestyle in general. In a way its a rejection of consumerism and the rise of consumer culture. People don't buy things that are made of good quality materials anymore. Instead they buy things that are trendy. Corporations who sell us this stuff have picked up on the trends as well. Products are designed to be obsolete in one or two years. Meanwhile newer products are constantly being pumped out for you the consumer to enjoy.

Living this way simply doesn't make sense. At its worst, consumer culture heightens our anxieties by creating a moving target for the ideal standard of living. Nothing will ever be enough. But you have the power to simply say no. To purchase things that you can use over and over for years. To repair old things as they break, and to spread awareness to everything that you own. The objects we use don't have to become obsolete.

Obsolescence implies the need to replace or get rid of. We should deal with obsolescence accordingly and not let it rule our decisions. Broken things are not meant to be in the house. Things that work but that are functionally useless should also simply go away. They exist like background noise only to distract you. Simply learning to let go brings many benedictions along the way. Obsolete objects represent the past, and letting go is like opening the door towards the future where better experiences and goals await you.

Finally there is the question of quantity and for how long these things should be cared for. The harmony of a house depends on a delicate balance of available space and placement of objects. Each object has an aura of usability. Too many objects causes disorder because we don't know what to do with them all. Nor do we begin to fathom when we will use them. These objects create a dead weight on well being. Suddenly the home isn't so beautiful. There is a disconnect between your needs and the content of objects.

Things are inanimate but they seem to have a life of their own. It is a life wrought out of relations to other objects. Neglect becomes visible on the surface of things, just like neglect of an animal shows in their eyes. Harmony isn't just within the home and within your mind, but in the objects themselves. Care for your things and make them last. They are in some sense, an extension of yourself and all the things that you do.

So continue on with this journey and see where exactly it takes you. Your purpose for reading this book may simply be to tidy up your living area. Or maybe you wanted a more theoretical explanation for why clutter happens and how to deal with it. This book provides ample direction for those who are interested. You may still wish to study up on things like mindfulness and the connection between thoughts and actions. The rest is up to you.

Printed in Great Britain
by Amazon

35466754R00099